THE ALSOLIFE

THE ALSOLIFE

BARBARA CAWTHORNE CRAFTON

Morehouse Publishing
NEW YORK · HARRISBURG · DENVER

Morehouse Publishing, 19 East 34th Street, New York, NY 10016

Morehouse Publishing is an imprint of Church Publishing Incorporated.
www.churchpublishing.org

Cover design by Laurie Klein Westhafer, Bounce Design
Typeset by Denise Hoff

Library of Congress Cataloging-in-Publication Data

Names: Crafton, Barbara Cawthorne, author.
Title: The alsolife / Barbara Cawthorne Crafton.
Description: New York : Morehouse Publishing, 2016. | Includes bibliographical references. | Description based on print version record and CIP data provided by publisher; resource not viewed.
Identifiers: LCCN 2016031881 (print) | LCCN 2016022297 (ebook) | ISBN 9780819232908 (ebook) | ISBN 9780819232892 (pbk.)
Subjects: LCSH: Christianity--Philosophy. | Ontology.
Classification: LCC BR100 (print) | LCC BR100 .C785 2016 (ebook) | DDC 230--dc23

LC record available at https://lccn.loc.gov/2016031881

Printed in the United States of America

CONTENTS

FOREWORD

We often say that God is the author of creation. Sometimes we even go so far as saying that God is present to all of us all the time. But I wonder if we really think through the implications of such claims that come so easily to people of faith? Because if God is everywhere and fully present in each moment and place of God's creation, then we are surrounded by witnesses to the nature of God wherever and whenever we look.

As an erstwhile scientist, a physicist who studied astrophysics and condensed matter, who now studies theology, I've marveled at the assertion that science and religion are in an unresolvable conflict. If we believe that God is the author of creation, there can be no rejection of scientific thinking by people of faith. As a scientist, I can be a person of faith, though

I have to be very careful that faith is not scientific, at least not in the way that science defines the word. (A discipline is scientific according to Karl Popper if it can make a claim that can be directly tested and shown to be either true or false. Under that criterion, faith is important and profound, but it's not science.)

It's striking how many people of faith hold scientific ideas at arm's length—perhaps afraid that the statements of faith will be subjected to the rigors of scientific inquiry and proved false. Since being able to prove something false would make it scientific and not a proper thing of faith after all, I don't quite think there's as much to fear as some imagine. That fear, however ungrounded, may keep us from fully embracing scientific ideas about the universe, about the nature of biology or of human origins. Some people of faith manage all this quite well, but a large number of faithful people across all traditions don't.

If we take our scientific ideas seriously, however, there is much that we begin to be able to say about God. This is the whole point of natural theology. Consider the question of time, for example. Such a simple thing on its surface, a thing we have been measuring for as long as humans have kept records, has physicists tied up in knots at the moment. Time in the universe seems to be mono-directional, always moving from past to present to future and never reversing. It can slow, it can stop, but almost all people will agree that it cannot reverse. But why? There's nothing in the basic equations that we write to describe the universe that should make it impossible to reverse time. In truth, the equations seem to demand that it be possible. And yet it isn't observed no matter where we look or how hard we try.

But there's more. Time seems to exist in some parts of the universe, but not in others. By not existing I mean that in the very beginning of the universe, before the explosion that we call the "Big Bang," and in the very distant future when the universe has expanded and expanded and expanded into simple elementary particles far separated from one another, time ceases to have any meaning. (In the distant future of the universe, there are no transitions from one thing to another, which are the way we think of time when we think of it in a non-abstract way. With no transitions, there are no seconds to count . . .)

Barbara writes of the difference between *chronos* time and *kairos* time in the book you're about to read. It's an old distinction, well known to students of theology and philosophy. And if you take the preceding paragraph seriously, the distinction between a series of transitions, the ticking of an atomic clock, and the idea of an eternal now isn't just a theological thought experiment. It's an essential part of a certain class of cosmological solutions to equations which describe our universe. In other words, by taking modern cosmology seriously, we've gotten ourselves a sure foundation for the sort of speculation that makes the writing of St. Augustine of Hippo so deeply fascinating.

This simple example—and there are many more that Barbara alludes to in the wonderful book you're holding—points us to an old idea. Natural theology is a pathway to understanding something about the nature of the God we worship. Rather than fearing scientific thought, or at best treating it with a wary suspicion, we ought to be waiting with bated breath for each new experimental result and, as theologians, trying to see which piece of this giant jigsaw puzzle it represents. There's a universe of meaning in each scientific observation, and that meaning points us to the handprints of God in God's creation.

A mystic is, at the simplest level, someone who sees a deeper reality in the experiences of daily life. If you apply this definition to scientists I've often thought that they are essentially mystics at heart. A scientist will work for years to extract a new insight from a simple physical observation, and if lucky, will use that insight to either reinforce, or perhaps build a new line of thinking about the interconnectedness of creation.

In this extended meditation, Barbara does the same sort of thing, but from the other side of the table. She uses insights gained from a life of faith, brings them into conversation with modern scientific thinking and tries to see how, once fitted together, the two create a ladder that takes us a little deeper into the presence of the God.

Enjoy the journey. And then go and do likewise as playfully and as seriously as you can.

—The Rt. Rev. W. Nicholas Knisely
XIII Bishop of the Diocese of Rhode Island

ACKNOWLEDGMENTS

This has been the most *collegial* of all my books—I've asked more people to read pieces of it than I can recall ever having done in the past. I must be getting old. Or maybe I'm just shedding some delusions of grandeur. If so, it's high time.

I took the train up to Providence to spend an hour with the good bishop of Rhode Island, Nick Knisely, who is both a physicist and a bishop. I don't know how many of those we have in the church; I think it's approximately one. It was a stimulating visit: I stammered out my ideas so he could tell me which ones were reasonable and which ones made no sense at all.

I never studied physics. I now think I would major in it if I were to go back to school today. Sometimes, I dream that

I am back in school, and that there is an exam in a class I have never bothered to attend. I have to take a heart pill when I wake up.

Another physicist who listened kindly to me was Patrick Davis, who is a brilliant church musician. We met at the Sewanee Church Music Conference. The participants of that conference endured several of my talks about the Alsolife, and for the most part they took it well. I thank them.

On second thought, I guess I'd major in art history. In my dotage, I have discovered a new vocation: sharing beautiful artwork and talking about it. You will endure a bit of this. I thank Douglas Blanchard, painter and professor of art history, who patiently answers all my questions and never makes me feel silly for asking them. Right now, the Almost-Daily eMos are practically nothing but art history lessons with a theological twist. It seems to agree with people. Sign up for them at www.geraniumfarm.org.

A picture is worth a thousand words, the saying goes, so I've included a few. They are all in the public domain.

Gordon Boals, Joan Castagnone, Sally Edwards, Henry Langhorne, Norah McCormack, Elizabeth Searle, Jane Smith, and Karen Stubaus all read chapters or worse and are still my friends. I needed some good minds—again, to tell me honestly if what I wrote was ridiculous. Henry kindly lent me one of his poems, inspired by this book. The faculty colloquium at the General Theological Seminary listened to me go on about this stuff for a solid hour one lunch period, to the same end. This, too, was most kind.

Deb Kmetz and Richard Quaintance—the famous Q—turned gimlet eyes upon the manuscript and found all my typos. Being a proofreader is something of a disease; it can make reading the newspaper pure anguish, to say nothing of the vapors such a person gets from billboards with misplaced apostrophes, more numerous with each passing day. But their disorder is essential to the writer's craft, and I am the beneficiary of it.

Nancy Bryan and Ryan Masteller of Church Publishing can take it from here. It is always a pleasure to work with them, and I am grateful for all they do to make it so easy.

I save the best for last. Corinna Crafton is the English teacher everybody should have. Her kindness and her curiosity about the universe brighten my days and gladden my heart, and her knowledge of literature beggars my own. She has added both breadth and depth to this book. If I thought I could rightly claim credit for her excellence, I would. But she left me in the dust long ago. Being her mother is a peculiar delight.

INTRODUCTION

Today, the newspaper was full of the news: gravitational waves have been detected and measured! After more than fifty years of trying, we have heard the sound of them. I myself heard it—on Facebook, of course—a steady rising tone with a little zip at the end and then, nothing. *Everything else in astronomy is like the eye. Finally, astronomy grew ears. We never had ears before,* said physicist Szabolics Marka, who is part of the scientific team that announced the discovery yesterday.

Oh, my. The bending of space-time. The disappearance of energy and matter in a collision of two colossally dense black holes. This was millions of years ago, maybe billions. And I heard it yesterday. I have thought about this, in my halting way, for years. Einstein elegantly predicted it, using mathematics I understand only dimly. For him and subsequent scientific generations it was a theory. And now, here it is.

That's what I love about science: It knows it's going to change. Even its mistakes are valuable; they are mileposts along the way of discovery. It can treasure its past without seeking to enshrine it. Religion has a harder time doing that. This book hopes to help it along. The witness of Scripture we hold to be inspired of God is a diverse witness. Ancient strands of different cultures, different languages, different eras combine in its pages. Each subsequent age has emphasized different strands; it is human nature to imagine that a local truth is a universal one.

Of course we have done this with our notion of what happens to us after we die. Most people wonder what the afterlife is like. I don't like that term, "afterlife"—it presupposes a linearity of time we now know not to be the whole truth.

I prefer my own word, *alsolife.* I'm offering it to our language as a new word.

The alsolife.

It is time to allow what we are learning about the nature of time to help us find the strength and hope that has been present in our tradition since it began, but which is not obvious to many people today. The ancient people who first wrote down the Scriptures and the ancient Christians who first observed the mystery of the Resurrection sensed that God was much more than a supernatural being. The idea that God is existence itself is not a newfangled notion. It is ancient.

Why does something so abstract as "God is existence itself" matter to you and to me? Because in the life we know, all of us lose everything. We can be comforted profoundly by a larger view. Does she still think of me? Does he miss me? The *alsolife* is a hopeful way of thinking about the ongoing life of the universe, in which the beloved dead and we ourselves all participate. It encourages us to go beyond our assumption that God is limited by time, as we are. Or that God is limited by anything else, for that matter. Pondering the *alsolife* will help you, I hope, when a loss overwhelms you to the point where you see little reason to go on. It has helped many with whom I have shared it.

Do not think that giving up our anthropomorphic ideas about God and heaven means that the life we know is all there is. Far from it.

So. This is not a book about science, since I am not a scientist, but there is science in it. This is not a book about art history, though it is full of art. I am not an art historian; I am an amateur (which—after all—means "lover"). This is not a book of poetry, since I am not a poet. But there is poetry in it. This is not a book about history, since I am not a historian, but there is history in it. This is not a book about psychology, since I am not a psychologist, but there is psychology in it.

This is a book about what might happen if we widened our view of what time is and what it is not. This is a book about human longing, human sorrow, and human hope, where they meet and become the energy of God.

—bcc+
Metuchen, New Jersey
2016

CHAPTER 1

SOME OF THE STARS ARE MISSING

A conversation:

Wow.

Yes. Impressive, aren't they?

Unbelievable.

And you haven't seen a fraction of them.

How many are there?

I don't count them.

But you make them.

We cause them, might be a better way of saying it.

We? How many of you are there?

One. But I don't count myself, either. There's no need.

It would take forever to count the stars.

Waste of time, too, By the time you finished, there would be a whole crop of new ones, and others would be gone, so you'd have to go back to the beginning. Besides, counting things is something only you people do. There's really no need.

Really? Somebody said that the numbers come from God and we discover the rest.

That was Pythagoras. A little before your time.

Did you know that he was the first to teach that the planets orbit the sun?

I did know that.

Can you see them all?

I am them all.

The stars are gods?

No. They can't be me, but I am them.

Wait . . . .

It's complicated.

I can't see you.

You don't have to. You are in me.

We don't see much in the way of stars in New York—well, we see plenty of celebrities, of course, but I mean stars in the sky. We might see the North Star. We might see Venus, down near the horizon. This summer Venus and Jupiter met and kept company for a while, which caused quite a stir. But mostly there's too much competition. When the entire city lost power in 1987 and again in 2003, the bridges filled each night with New Yorkers, gazing up in wonder at the night sky. Many of them had never seen so many stars. We have substantially more than our share of ambient light here. The stars literally pale by comparison.

It is not so in the country. Walking in the dark one Friday night at Holy Cross Monastery, an hour up the Hudson River from the city, I could barely find my way to the guest house from the parking lot. I wondered uneasily if it were true that bears had been seen with increasing frequency thereabouts and if one of them might not at that moment be making his way over to the monastery's garbage cans to enjoy some of the brothers' supper leftovers. But when I happened to glance upward, I stopped in my tracks, forgetting all about the bears: the stars were so bright, the sky so black. And there were so *many* stars, and they so seemed to lean right out of heaven toward me, as if I could have reached up and plucked one. I stood there for a long time. Finally I managed to tear myself away from that overwhelming beauty and went inside. I wanted to tell somebody what I had seen, but it was late. The house was in silence. I climbed the stairs to my room on the third floor and went to bed. I was still happy about it as sleep found me—there were so many stars, and they were so beautiful.

They are far away, the stars. The light emanating from them must travel billions of miles, billions upon billions, before it meets my eye. Even at the speed of light, the journey of a star's light to my eye takes a long, long time. Millions of years.

Billions of years. By the time I experience it, it may well have ended its existence. It may have gone on to whatever next act awaits a twinkling star—the red giant phase, perhaps, or the white dwarf. It may be in the process of blowing up. Or it may have done so already, and may now be imploding, shrinking down and down into a dense darkness capable of sucking into itself anything that comes near. Whatever it is doing, it is not doing now what I see it doing now, twinkling in the sky. That moment is over.

So I am not seeing that star as it is when I see it. I am seeing it as it was. I am seeing that star's past, in my present.

I am seeing that star's past *in my present.*

But wait—it is not quite right to say that the moment I behold is over. It cannot be over, not if I am beholding it. Though it is no longer true for that star in that place at that time, it is true for me, in my space and time. Both moments are true. The past and the present exist simultaneously. And if that is so, the future must also be there. My future is someone else's present, someone else's past. All my eras exist. They just do so at different times.

This is the *alsolife*. This must be what existence in time and space is for God. Christianity in the West has made much of our God as a God of history, and has expected God's will to find expression in what happens there. But, though the work of God can be discerned in history, it cannot be true that the God of history is *contained* in history—it must be the other way around. *He's got the whole world in his hands*, goes the old spiritual, and in its simplicity it speaks a profound truth: All events in history are contained in God. Nothing is outside of God's time or outside of God's existence. If there were a time outside of God—beyond God, before God, after God, other than God—then we would not be talking about God, would we? God must be, as Paul put it, "all in all."

Let us switch places. Now we are on one of the planets orbiting that faraway star, looking back at the earth. We are using the telescopes that planet's inhabitants have developed, which are far superior to any we have, and so we can see the neighborhood clearly, and in great detail. There's your house, and your cat in the yard. There's your neighbor, working in his garden. There's your teenager, texting somebody on her phone. *This is some telescope,* you might say to your extraterrestrial host, and he would lower his seven eyes modestly and say it was nothing, really.

But by the time we see all this, your teenager and your cat and your neighbor have been gone for years. Millennia. Eons. Your house is gone. The earth is gone. The sun may be gone, too. By the time we visitors to that distant planet behold your neighborhood through our fancy borrowed telescope, it has all been gone for a long, long time. We are looking in the present of our location in space, but that is not what we are seeing. We may be looking in the present, but we are seeing the past.

Think of it: In such an extreme, imaginary look through a telescope that may not exist, we would peer into the past. Someone else, I suppose, in some other faraway place, could have been looking at us at the same moment, and the present in which we were living would be that being's past, too. *When* it was would have a lot to do with *where* it was.

Go to an Easter vigil, late at night on Holy Saturday. A fire is kindled in the dark. It is called the "new fire." A fresh paschal candle, as beautifully ornamented as the parish can afford, is brought to the priest, who may prepare it by inserting five red nails into the cross incised in the wax. "Christ," the priest says, inserting the nails one by one, "Yesterday, today, and tomorrow. The Beginning and the End. The First and the Last. He is the Alpha and the Omega. His are the times and His the seasons. To Him be glory, forever and ever." Then the priest lights the candle from the new fire, and the central liturgy of the Christian year begins once more.

The Great Vigil of Easter, then, which marks Christ's crossing from death to life, is also a liturgy about time. In the Easter Vigil, the past is brought forward into the present. The creation of the world, and the terror of its inundation. The central miracle of the Hebrew people in their deliverance at the Red Sea. The devastating conundrum of how Abraham is to relate to God, posed unthinkably in the aborted sacrifice of his son. The fanciful re-membering of the dry bones that Ezekiel saw. The hope and the glimpse of life beyond the boundaries of the life we know. These stories are told again, slowly unfolding once more. The Easter Vigil is not a service for people in a hurry. It takes time to tell all the stories.

When the Vigil begins, we are still tired and sore from Good Friday. It soaked us in history and death: a specific martyrdom, in a specific city, at a specific time. A specific man. Political and religious leaders whose names we know: Pontius Pilate, Caiaphas, Annas. Dense psychological accretions of centuries cling to Good Friday—combining with our exhaustion, they threaten to reduce the Crucifixion either to a tale about a monstrous political injustice or a fable about our personal misdeeds. But although the Passion narratives have been host to both ideas in later centuries, neither of them is complete on its own. The stories of the Vigil widen our focus, reminding us of *everything* that has made us what we are: the beauty, the love, the terror, the betrayal, the hope. In the darkness, lit only by candles, the stories locate themselves in a matrix larger than any one place or time. It is as if we soared high above the surface of the earth, beholding all its beauties and all its sorrows. Our faith isn't just about a wrongful death, nor is it about an essentially mercantile exchange of one innocent Victim for an entire race of the guilty. It is also about the life beyond the boundaries of the life we know, the beating down not only of death, but of the ache of time. The only reason time hurts us at all is that it brings us closer to death—our own death, and the death of all we have loved. To know our provincial experience of linear time as part of a continuity, rather than the whole of what time is, is to begin to break free of its sting.

Listen:

When you were in school and began to study history, your teacher used a time line to help you locate important events and eras in their chronological order. If you were a child in the Western Hemisphere, the line began over on the left side of the blackboard with the beginning of the world. Then came plants and animals, simple one-celled life forms first, growing in complexity as the eons passed, up through dinosaurs and wooly mammoths and into the species we now know. Then humankind appeared, first as hunter-gatherers and then as farmers. City dwellers. The Hebrews and the pyramids and the Roman Empire. The birth of Christ. The Jewish diaspora. The conversion of Constantine, then the fragmentation of the Roman world and the centuries of the medieval era. The Renaissance and the age of exploration. On and on the line went, through wars, monarchs, inventions, disasters, ending in an arrow at the far right, pointing toward forever. The time line helped you in history class, helped you remember who came first, Columbus or Magellan (it was Columbus). If your school days were long ago, the time line had some important pieces missing, and you are still not sure when the Han Dynasty ruled China, and whether or not it coincided with the Chola Dynasty in India (it didn't).

We remember that line. We still find it useful. We reproduce it when we remember our own lives. *Let's see*, we say, trying to place something, *that was before Mom died, because she was there* or *Let's see, that must have been during the war, because we still had those awful dark shades on all the windows.* We remember our lives in a line, a before-and-after linear progression of events. Linear time seems manifestly true to us, so obvious a fact as not to be worth mentioning.

But we are startled, sometimes, when we experience time in some other way. Almost always, our time line works, but there are occasions upon which it does not. The phenomenon of déjà vu is one—that eerie moment when you know what someone will say before she says it, and then she does. *Well, that was weird,* you think to yourself. It never lasts more than a moment or two, and then it is gone. It is not a frequent occurrence, but it is likely that most people have experienced déjà vu at least once in their lives. What is it?

An abundance of studies in neuroscience have offered explanations of déjà vu, none of which begin with anything like the idea that it might be an experience of something that is actually happening—that time itself might be elastic and relative to the position and experience of the subject. Perhaps that is an approach that should at least be considered: perhaps déjà vu should not automatically be considered an illusion. Knowing what we now know about the elasticity of our experience of time, it seems reasonable to factor this knowledge into our attempts to understand such a well-known human phenomenon. Perhaps déjà vu really *is* an instance in which we become unmoored in time for a moment. Perhaps, for a moment, we grasp the simultaneity of events in the whole dominion of God, in which past, present, and future are all one thing. Perhaps it is not a mistake at all, but rather a glimpse of a larger reality we are ordinarily unable to experience. Albert Einstein famously said that time is what we have so that everything doesn't happen all at once. But it may be that everything *does* happen all at once, and that linear time is merely the neurological model we create in order to accommodate our limited brains.

Perhaps linear time is earthly, and not cosmic: applicable only here, and not in the larger life that religious people call the kingdom of God. *Humankind cannot bear very much reality,* T. S. Eliot wrote, and it is so.[1]

You fall asleep and dream. In your dream, you are in your bedroom in your childhood home—but you are the age you are now. You hear your father downstairs, hear the clatter of cups and saucers as he prepares the tea for breakfast. Your father has been dead for many years, and in your dream you know this—but you go downstairs to the kitchen and there he is anyway, wearing the old grey cardigan he always wore at home, the teapot in his hands. Little is said between you—conversation seems not to be the purpose of this encounter. The two of you have become unmoored in time for a moment, breaching the walls of your separate spheres, bridging the gap between the living and the dead. You awaken, bemused. It seemed so real.

It was only a dream. You know that, after a few waking seconds.

But who are we to say a dream is not real? The ancients believed wholeheartedly in the power of God to speak to human beings in dreams. An impoverished modern definition of truth over the last three hundred years or so—one that sought to reduce reality to mere measurable fact—dismissed this possibility. More recently, though, we have found it possible to recover some lost ground. Might there be more to dreams than illusion, after all? Must our dreams be, of necessity, only misplaced fragments of our waking reality and nothing more? Neuropsychology knows them to be the figurative and symbolic work of the part of the brain that thinks in pictures, symbols, puns, and metaphors—the part that becomes active while the list-making, analytical part of the brain takes a break. We

1 T. S. Eliot, "Burnt Norton," in *The Four Quartets* (1935).

know that this part of us also considers the stuff of our lives, in its way. *Why don't you sleep on it,* someone says about a knotty problem, and we awaken the next day with a fresh insight. No, your dream is not real like your second-period class will be real later on this morning. But it may be real in another way—real, but not part of the linear arrangement upon which we habitually depend to order our reality. What if your dream is an experience of another dimension that cuts across the ones through which we ordinarily see things, the dimensions of time and space?

Philosophers and theologians speak of time using two different Greek words: *chronos* and *kairos*. *Chronos* is the time of the earth, the passing of seconds and minutes, hours, weeks, years, millennia. *Chronos* is about duration. How long does it take? How long have you been here? How long is it until supper time? *Chronos* is the time of the time line in school.

The other word for time is *kairos*. *Kairos* is the time of God. Sometimes it breaks into our chronological world. The Bible describes such moments in various ways: the appointed time, the fullness of time, the right time, the time fulfilled. *Kairos* contains *chronos* but is not bound by it. *Chronos* can never contain *kairos,* but it can be reshaped by it.

The physics of our era describes the elasticity of time, introducing us all to the slippery idea that things don't exist in time and space except in relation to other things. All of us, and everything else that exists, does so in space-time, and our location in space-time is dependent upon one another's location. *When* I am is relative to *where* I am, and the reverse is also true. In travel through space we will see this, if we ever travel far enough and fast enough: time on the spacecraft will pass in the usual earthly way. The ship's clocks will still work, the digital calendars will still mark the days, which will still be twenty-four hours long. When we come home, though, we will discover that the days that were twenty-four hours long for us on the ship were somehow longer here, that our dear ones will have grown older than we have. We will be like Rip Van Winkle awakening after his long sleep, which seemed to him but an afternoon's nap: We will return to a world profoundly changed, unrecognizable to us. And it won't just *seem* so; it will really *be* so. The absolute categories of a Newtonian world fall short of describing the whole picture of the universe—they work well enough here on the earth, but they don't work everywhere all of the time. Time on the earth is really a measure of change, and change requires that something be lost: I went to college and therefore was no longer in high school. I married, and therefore was no longer single. My hair turned grey and I was no longer a blonde. That was then and this is now. *Chronos. Chronos* is a measure of loss.

But then and now must *both* be present still, in the larger domain of God. Nothing can be absent from God. In the domain of God, there can be no *duration*. Things just *are*. In *kairos*, nothing is lost.

He's got the whole world in his hands. Nothing is truly simultaneous in *chronos*. When I speak to you and you answer, my question is already in the past. When I climb the stairs the step from which I just lifted my foot is in the past, and my next step is in the future. The two steps are close together in time, but they are not the same moment. *Chronos*.

For God, it must be different. Everything must be simultaneous in God's time. There can be no past from which God is absent, no future that fails to include God. God is the one who includes the cosmos; it cannot be the other way around. When we speak of God, we are dealing with something much more like a sphere than like a line. We stand in the center and find ourselves equidistant from every point on the surface. God is all around us. This is an existence which encompasses us but which we cannot encompass, an existence we can never leave. The dominion of God is existence itself. Further, the dominion of God cannot be separated from the divine self—just as God cannot have the before-and-after limit of duration, so God cannot have the not-here-but-there limit of location. God can't live anywhere, so God must live everywhere. For God, matter and energy are, at bottom, different forms of the same thing or, as Einstein put it succinctly, $E = MC^2$. Energy is actually matter moving really fast! The creation is a burst of energy, which is ongoing. It becomes everything that is. There is nothing outside it.

Who are you? Moses wanted to know four thousand years ago, and we have been wrestling with this reasonable question ever since. For some of us, it has led to conundrum upon conundrum as we have created intricate structures of thought about God, edifices that soared far above the experiences of human life. But Moses doesn't ask a speculative question. Freeing the Hebrews from their enslavement will be a formidable task, and he wants to know who will undergird his response. Is he on his own, or does he have backup?

> Then Moses said to God, "If I come to the people of Israel and say to them, 'The God of your fathers has sent me to you,' and they ask me, 'What is his name?' what shall I say to them?" God said to Moses, "I am who I am." And he said, "Say this to the people of Israel, 'I AM has sent me to you.'"[2]

The God of their fathers is one thing, a concrete memory—surely most of the Israelites to whom Moses must make his case will remember at least *some* of the stories about Abraham, Isaac, and Jacob. The Name, though, is something else entirely.

2 Exod 3:13–14.

I AM? What is that supposed to mean? *You want us to leave everything we know here to follow—what? A sentence fragment?* I am often tempted to see interpolation when Scripture doesn't make sense, the work of a later hand trying to make the record a little more plausible. I do think I see it here, especially when I consider the absurdly anthropomorphic God Moses encounters only ten verses later:

> At a lodging place on the way the Lord met him and sought to kill him.[3]

Good grief.

Some ancient writer may have been interested in deepening Moses's experience of God for us. His project has been successful—the God of the Exodus isn't just the folkloric partisan of the Israelites whom we meet in this story. God is existence itself. And, while the sophisticated *I AM* response to Moses may be a newer addition, it is far from modern. Somebody in very ancient times thought God was much more than a partisan deity who might lie in ambush to kill Moses. God was existence itself.

Theologians may ask speculative questions about God, but most people have more personal reasons for inquiring into the divine nature. Theology is interesting all the time, but it becomes urgent to us when loss threatens. How can we get free? What will the death I am facing mean? For that matter, what did my life mean? Will I ever see her again? Will I get a second chance? Does pain go on forever? It is these existential cries that rise heavenward. When we speak of such things as the elasticity of time, the identity between energy and matter, the absence of duration and location, are we speaking of anything that will make it more possible for us to live in peace of

3 Exod. 3:24.

spirit? Are these means by which the power that creates the universe can "incarnate" for us in a way that our minds can handle, enough for us to touch it just a bit? Or even just to *imagine* touching it? Or are these just interesting puzzlements, the parlor games of a religious temperament—literally, of no earthly good?

No. This is more than a game.

Our losses resound throughout our lives. They are the reason our exploration of time matters.

CHAPTER 2

FREUD DISCOVERS THE CITY OF TROY

The latter half of the nineteenth century and the first few decades of the twentieth were a golden age of archeological exploration. This was the era that saw the excavation of the Valley of the Kings and the stupendous tomb of Tutankhamen, the discovery of the Minoan civilization, of the Mayan and Aztec empires, and the stunning cave paintings of old Europe. The intelligentsia of Europe and America were thrilled by this energetic contact with the ancient world. Popular culture expressed the excitement of these discoveries, as well: the flowing Isidora Duncan–style garments fashionable women wore, the popularity of Egyptian revival furniture, the ubiquity of vaguely Oriental-looking table legs and armrests, china, cutlery, textiles, and even teapots—everyone wanted them.

Visit Sigmund Freud's rooms in Vienna. You can—they are now a museum. You can see his waiting room, the famous couch upon which his famous patients reclined, the chair in which he sat, outside their range of vision as they talked, the wide window looking out upon the sidewalk in front of famous *Bergasse 19*. Certainly Freud enjoyed his own eminence: He wanted to defer the publication of his seminal *The Interpretation of Dreams* until the year 1900, so that he could be remembered as the greatest mind of the twentieth century, and not the nineteenth. The couch and the chair command their share of bemusement for the visitor, but what is immediately striking are the antiquities that fill the place. Freud

Freud's "audience"[1]

1 Photograph by Edmund Engelman, May 1938. It was part of a careful photographic session just before Freud fled Vienna to escape the Nazi occupation, with the intention of re-creating his rooms after the war was over, as a museum. Freud died in England, in September of 1939.

began his collecting after the death of his father and continued for forty years, until he himself died. Famously ambivalent throughout his life about his own Jewish heritage, he focused in his collecting on other cultures—Egyptian, Greek, Chinese. There are scores of them, hundreds of them: tiny Mesopotamian deities, seated Egyptian gods and goddesses, Greek and Roman busts, fragments of funeral mosaics and masks, ancient little animals and birds, urns, plates, chalices. A line of such figures stands on the edge of Freud's desk, silent witnesses to his treatment notes; Freud referred to them as "my audience."

What you see in the apartment now is only a fraction of what Freud amassed—he was a passionate collector, seeking out dealers in every city he visited. In this interest, he was a man of his time, eagerly devouring every new discovery of the ancient world.

One discovery in particular fascinated Freud: Heinrich Schliemann's excavation of the traditional site of Troy, city of the *Iliad*, which had begun in the 1870s and continued sporadically even after Schliemann's death in 1890 for another century and more. Before Schliemann, most people assumed that the Homeric epics were works of pure fiction, ancient legend but not historical fact. Most assumed that the people we encounter there—Agamemnon, Clytemnestra, Priam, Hector, Paris—were fictional characters, the stuff of legend and nothing more. The traditional site of Troy was just that: a tradition. None of this was real. The *Iliad* was just a story.

But Schliemann and a few other enthusiasts believed otherwise. Who was to say that Troy was only a legend? What if Agamemnon and the others were *not* just characters in an old story, but real people, real places? What if the island Ithaka was *not* just named after the legendary home of wily Odysseus, but had that name before blind Homer told his tale? What if Troy were real? What if it had lain buried for centuries under the dusty plain of Hisarlik, in what is now Turkey? Possessed of a fortune he had made in the indigo trade, Schliemann was able to finance his own expedition, and he began to dig.

Later archeologists have taken issue with Schliemann's excavating technique: Eager to find the city he was sure was down there, he tore through meter after meter and layer after layer of ancient history, destroying precious artifacts as he went. But archeology was hardly even in its infancy then. Whatever his errors, Schliemann can be credited with the discovery of the Mycenaean civilization and the actual city of Troy. He did not find just one Troy, either: City upon city had been built in the same location, each one erected upon the rubble of the one preceding it. There were nine altogether, one on top of the other, from the rugged surface of nineteenth-century Hisarlik down through medieval towns, through the Bronze Age city all the way down to the discarded animal bones and broken drinking cups of the hunter-gatherers who first came there. Schliemann thought the lowest of the cities, Troy Level IX, must be Homer's Troy, having found a remarkable trove of gold jewelry there, which he smuggled out of Turkey in a pillowcase.

Schleimann's wife, Sophia Engastromenos, wearing the "Jewels of Helen."

They are now in the Pushkin Museum in Moscow. This remains a sore point with the Turks.

This he christened "Priam's Treasure," and a photograph survives of Schliemann's pretty young wife wearing much of it: a gold headdress, many gold necklaces and dangling earrings. Later scholars have ascertained that this was not *that* Troy at all, that the treasure was not Priam's but someone else's, and went to some pains to straighten out the confusion caused by Schliemann's hasty digging. In this they have been successful, and ascertained that the Troy of the *Iliad* is Troy Level VI.

Schliemann had a flair for self-promotion. He sent frequent dispatches about his discoveries to newspapers of record throughout the world to keep his name before the public. Schliemann did more than anyone theretofore to ensure for the field of archeology a permanent place in the popular imagination. People everywhere waited eagerly for news of what might be unearthed next at Troy.

Freud, too, was thrilled with the Troy discoveries. Besides firing his collector's zeal, the strata of cities fascinated him for a reason that went far beyond his interest in old things. Messy as Schliemann's technique had been, Troy was still the first mound on dry land to be excavated in a systematic way. The dig exposed the cities in layers, like a cake. Slice it vertically, and all nine Troys were visible at once, one century upon another, upon another, upon yet another. Freud saw at once that the human psyche was like that, too, with one important difference: all the levels were still alive! It was as if people still lived in all the layered cities, still ate and drank, still made love, sold real estate, argued, wove rugs, shoed horses—all alive, all accessible, all living their human lives. The experiences of a person's life remain. The past lives in the present. As William Faulkner would put it, years later, "The past isn't dead. It isn't even past."

Try to put a turtleneck top on your one-year-old. She pitches a fit about it. Her distress is extreme, beyond what it's worth, you think as you struggle to pull it over her head. But it reminds her of another tight fit, one that happened not that long ago. Babies remember head compression, and they don't like it.

Go to a cocktail party where you don't know anyone. Suddenly, you're a fourteen-year-old wallflower again. You dread going up to some stranger and making small talk. You can't wait to leave.

Enter an elevator. Someone is wearing Chanel No. 5. You look around for your mother, who has been dead since 1980.

Somebody wants you to find something on a road map. You feel a bit sick to your stomach. Your parents used to argue about the route on Sunday drives, and their vehemence frightened you.

Your father had to go to meetings at night when you were three. You wept uncontrollably each time he left the house. He had not been there when you were born; he was overseas then. Even now, you feel nervous and sad when your husband leaves the house to go out in the evening.

Everybody knows about these things.

The past isn't dead. It isn't even past.

The past is alive in our present.

The unearthing of past trauma was the centerpiece of Freud's work with patients. As with Schliemann, so with Freud: Later practitioners of his art dissented on many aspects of his approach. But both were pioneers—it would fall, as it always does, to later generations to redact their contributions to human knowledge. Freud was a great admirer of Schliemann, and compared himself to the archeologist on several occasions.

> Imagine that an explorer arrives in a little-known region where his interest is aroused by an expanse of ruins, with remains of walls, fragments of columns, and tablets with half-effaced and unreadable inscriptions. He may content himself with inspecting what lies exposed to view, with questioning the inhabitants—perhaps semi-barbaric people—who live in the vicinity, about what tradition tells them of the history and meaning of these archaeological remains, and with noting down what they tell him—and he may then proceed on his journey. But he may act differently. He may have brought picks, shovels and spades with him, and he may set the inhabitants to work with these implements. Together with them he may start upon the ruins, clear away the rubbish, and, beginning from the visible remains, uncover what is buried.[1]

I forget now what prompted me to explore Freud's admiration of Schliemann, his excitement over the discoveries at Hisarlik, his immediate appreciation for what some have called the "master metaphor" for his work. But I was struck immediately, as Freud was, by the power of this analogy for *my* life's work, which is the human attempt to discern God's presence in the world. If Troy is an apt metaphor for the layered human psyche, it is also richly suggestive when we try to understand what time might be for God. For us, the layered cities of time are buried once they have taken their places in the past. For God, they are laid bare. God sees them all, in all the stages of their life. Everything is alive at the same time. Everything is present. If there is anything hidden from

1 Sigmund Freud, "The Aetiology of Hysteria" (lecture, Vienna College of Psychiatry and Neurology, April 1896).

the eye of God, we cannot be talking about God. *For there is nothing hidden that will not be disclosed, and nothing concealed that will not be known or brought out into the open.*[2]

Holding all our times and seasons, but unbounded by any of them. Nothing can be truly simultaneous on the earth—what is plain to see when the distances are vast (as they were in our imaginary gaze back at our earthly home from the distant star) is also true when the distances are small. Whether we can detect it or not, there is always the tiniest distance between objects, always the tiniest of journeys to be made between an event and our experience of it. Here under the sun, we can never be more than next to each other. But in the dominion of God, the distance between us, one from another, is overcome at last. Our isolation is over. Paul speaks often of our being "in Christ." Not near Christ. Not next to Christ. *In* Christ.

I remember a seminary class in the Resurrection narratives. The professor stunned me when he suggested that our resurrection will be just like that of Jesus. This seemed blasphemous to me—I will be the *same* as *Jesus*? He won't be far *above* me? How can *that* be? I had a hard time getting past the vision of resurrected life I had inherited, that heaven would be a permanent version of an ancient imperial court. There would be a throne and we would worship the one who sat on it—that had been my vision. Certainly, it explained why people don't work any harder than they do to get there. This was different. Now, I was being asked to entertain the idea that there are no thrones in heaven at all. Interesting. I was not an unsophisticated student. I read liberation theology and process theology and sacramental theology and several other theologies whose names I cannot now remember. Perhaps I might surrender the throne itself, accepting it as metaphor

2 Luke 8:17.

rather than fact. So all right—maybe heaven was not like a long church service. But would the resurrection eliminate the distance between myself and the Son of God? Surely not.

That was before I learned that I didn't know our tradition as well as I thought I did.

CHAPTER 3

THE KINGDOM OF HEAVEN IS

You can find the Last Judgment in any old European church, and you won't have to look very hard for it. It will be in some prominent place, so nobody can miss it. It may be a fresco on a wall. The judgment may be carved in stone on the space above the west door. Or it may be outside, over the lintel at the entrance. But it's there somewhere, that's for sure.

The year is 1028, or 1265, or 1379. It is the Lord's Day, and you are in church. The Mass is in Latin. The homily is in Latin. The hymns and Scripture readings—all in Latin. You are French. You neither speak nor read Latin. Truth to tell, you don't read French either, and it doesn't matter. You are a blacksmith, as was your father before you and his father before him. Your son will be a blacksmith. There is no opportunity, nor is there any need, for anybody you know to learn how to read. If something important comes down from the king or from the pope, the priest will read it out to everyone.

But you know all the stories. The pictures in the windows of the cathedral, in the carvings over the west door, in the triptych behind the altar, in the frescoes on the walls—these teach you the stories every week. You know about Adam and Eve and Noah and Moses. You know about Lot's wife and Balaam's ass. You know Mary and Elizabeth and Joseph and most of the apostles. And you know about the Last Judgment. You believe in it.

Pieter van der Heyden, 1558

All depictions of the Last Judgment are more or less the same: Jesus is enthroned at the top, surrounded by the righteous. They may be at his right hand, or they may be in a circle around him. They are dressed more or less the same, in white robes. Often they are singing, their mouths identical round Os. Although I suppose they are impressive in their orderliness, they are not the most interesting people in the painting. Those would be the damned—and there are many more of them. Their world is more chaotic, so they take up more space.

The damned are having a terrible time in hell. Grinning demons torture them in imaginative ways: they are impaled on pitchforks, pulled apart limb from limb, buried headfirst in reeking mud. Some swim desperately in sulfurous lakes of fire, while others shiver, naked, in frigid dark caves. They are hideously raped by demons. Some of them appear to be getting more or less what they ordered in life: the greedy must swallow streams of golden coins excreted by demons into their open mouths, for instance, and the gluttonous must consume enormous plates of some unidentifiable putrescence. The adulterous are chained to their partners in illicit love and must stay that way through eternity—you can tell by their facial expressions that this is hard on the relationship.

The pictures on the cathedral wall are intended to terrify you into behaving yourself.

This is the hell of Dante. It is the hell of Giotto, his contemporary. This, or some version of it, is the hell we have inherited. For Dante, hell is a very local place. He knows who is there: Many of its denizens are his political enemies in thirteenth-century Florence, and Dante names names. This grim certainty, too, we have inherited: Many a Christian would sooner give up his hope of heaven than surrender his vision of hellfire and damnation for those of whom he disapproves. Dante's famous poem is composed of three parts—*Inferno, Purgatorio,* and *Paradiso*—but hardly anybody who is not a scholar ever reads the second two. It is hell that catches and holds our attention. The history of Western art owes a tremendous debt to this perverse predilection of ours: You could endow your way out of your just deserts by commissioning artwork for a church or by building one from scratch, and many a wealthy sinner did just that.

But all that was a long time ago. Why do people cling to a medieval vision of hell *now*? Why do we continue to believe in it centuries later, long after we stopped buying indulgences to mitigate the consequences of our misdeeds? *Well, hell is right there in the Bible,* someone might answer indignantly, and so it is, though Dante's ornate Inferno bears scant resemblance to the biblical writers' fleeting mentions of hell. But there are many things "in the Bible" we do *not* treasure, many things we simply ignore—we've gotten beyond stoning adulterers and silencing women in church, we've managed to soften our pastoral approach to divorce and remarriage, managed to forget all about honoring the Sabbath and about the prohibition against charging interest on loans. We've managed to dispense with whole lists of dietary laws and purity codes from the Hebrew Scriptures. We have found ways to explain such changes to ourselves in a manner that has enabled us to feel consistent with our tradition. But still, some of us insist on a literal understanding of eternal damnation, and imagine that a loving God is willing to consign us to it if we don't behave.

Later, we will turn our attention in some detail to issues of justice. For now, though, it is enough to note that the notion of eternal punishment also functions as a means by which we attempt to satisfy our longing for justice. There are many unrighted wrongs in the world, and this offends us. The neat economy of reward and punishment that heaven and hell provide appeals to us—it punishes those whom we cannot punish ourselves, and restores what the righteous have lost. We want this symmetry so much that we are willing to overlook the unlikely parochialism of such a vision of God, conditioned as it is by both time and location. Hell probably isn't really all about thirteenth-century Florence. Heaven probably isn't full of your dead relatives, either, looking just as they did here, except with wings. For now, though, let us defer balancing the scales of justice, and consider the present reality of the dominion of God.

The Jesus of whom the gospel writers speak comes to us through the Greek language in which they wrote. The Greek of Matthew, Mark, Luke, John, and also of Paul was richer and yet more economical in the grammar of speaking about the progression of events than our English is. When we remember what we were taught about tenses in school, we are likely to equate "tense" with "time." Mostly, this is pretty straightforward: things either were or are or they will be. But the way the biblical writers thought was different: They were not so much writing when an action occurs as about how complete the action is. They weren't in our grammar school history class, with its time line on the chalkboard. The location of events along that line was not as central a fact to them as it is to us.

So Jesus speaks about the kingdom of heaven in a way that seems to us to lack precision. Is it a current reality, or is it in the future, we ask impatiently, wanting to pin him down. But he does not share our temporal anxiety. *The kingdom of heaven IS like a mustard seed . . . IS like yeast . . . IS like a man who sowed a field . . . IS like a merchant looking for pearls . . . IS like a fishing net.* Is, is, is—Jesus speaks as if the kingdom is now. And yet he lives, as we also live, in a world riddled with sorrow. This is manifestly NOT the kingdom of heaven, we say, pointing to this or that egregious fact of life. So is the kingdom now, or is it in the future?

We briefly considered the paradoxical bending of time already, when we thought about the stars and how we experience them: how we are able, from our present, to behold the stars' past. Already we have begun to wean ourselves from the exclusivity of linear time, able to consider (though we find it difficult to imagine) an existence within which it does not apply. When we think of God in history, the beginnings and endings by which we mark our lives fail to account for the eternity of God. God can't have a beginning or an ending. The more we think, the more we begin to see a God who is looking less and less like an old white man with a beard and more and more like existence itself.

We imagine ourselves to be ever so much smarter than the biblical writers—they lived so long ago, and they didn't have the Internet. But, though there were many facts of which they were unaware, they did possess a richer way of thinking than we allow ourselves. We are apt to think that the way we are is the only way anything could be. It is hard for us to admit that anything could be beyond the reach of our minds, since we have grasped so much already—if we don't understand something now, we're sure that we soon will. With far more mysteries in their lives than we have, they were more humble than we are. We should not let the fact that they constructed folkloric metaphors to express their mysteries count against our assessment of their intelligence. They knew they were expressing ineffable things in mythic terms. With many more demonstrable facts at our disposal, we are yet no better than they were at expressing the ineffable. When we try, we quickly lose all concrete sense of what we're talking about.

> In the beginning was the Word, and the Word was with God, and the Word was God. He was in the beginning with God; all things were made through

> him, and without him was not anything made that was made.[1]

The meaning of this passage is not luminously clear. It wasn't then, either. We turn as quickly as we can to the Baby Jesus, so that we can talk about things we already know. But the fact that the mysteriously hymnic beginning of the gospel of John is in our Bibles, the book having survived the church's lengthy political process of deciding which of the earliest writings would make it into the canon of Scripture and which would not—in meetings that probably would have made your most acrimonious diocesan convention look like a Sunday school picnic—means that they spoke to at least some of the early Christians, and that their number and influence was sufficient to carry weight in a decision-making body.

Our Scripture is not less holy to us because we know a fair amount about its composition and compilation. It need not have been discovered buried somewhere in upstate New York, like the book of Mormon, or recited to Mohammed by the angel Gabriel, like the Koran. Our Bible was written by human beings whose activity spanned a thousand years and several different cultural and linguistic groups, inspired by God to use the brains God gave them in an attempt to communicate their experience of God. They were doing in their eras, with the tools at hand, what we must do in ours, with our own tools: find a way to embrace and communicate the meaning of God's presence in the world, our presence here, and the basis for a moral path. This is why errors and inconsistencies in Scripture are not troubling to us—"inspired by God" doesn't mean "inerrant," as "dictated by God" would. So the cumbersome process of explaining away inconsistencies in Scripture is unnecessary, as are humiliating decisions against common sense, decisions taken in order

1 John 1:1–3.

that one might believe. We no longer live in a world in which we must demand that of ourselves.

We know about its compilation, as well. The Roman destruction of the temple at Jerusalem in 70 CE and the resultant scattering of the Jewish people throughout Europe, Africa, and Asia meant that the essential fact of worship life could no longer be centered on animal sacrifice in a central sanctuary, as it had been for hundreds of years. All they had now was what they could carry with them: their holy scriptures and the majesty of the law. A group of rabbis living in Jabneh, together with other rabbis who visited them periodically, left a record of discussions concerning which books, already read as scripture, should still be considered as such. Christian historians have romanticized these conversations as the "Council of Jamnia [Jabneh]," dating it in 90 CE, as if it were a single council like the council of Nicea, but such a suggestion conflates a Jewish process with later Christian ones. Rabbinical visits to Jabneh for discussions of scripture there and other such discussions in other places continued long after 90 CE, and no binding list of authoritative books emerged from that or any other city. It seems that the rabbis' main purpose in these gatherings was to hash out the implications of the texts themselves. Rather than looking at Jabneh as a "council," consider it a part of the Talmudic process, the ongoing argument that produced Jewish thought and sustains it to this day.

The process of codifying the Christian scriptures was similarly long, though they were substantially agreed upon by the time of the Council of Nicea in 386—the makeup of the canon was not on the table there. Just as in the controversies of Paul's day in the mid-first century, the Jewishness of the early church remained a hot topic. Of great interest was the question of whether or not the Hebrew scriptures should be included in the Christian canon. Of course they should, Jewish Christians asserted; Jesus is the fulfillment of prophecy. How will people know that if they don't read it? Christians from a Greek background saw it differently—Jesus may indeed have been the fulfillment of Hebrew prophecy, but they were busy finding him in their own heritage. People in the first century inhabited two worlds at once: that of their own birth and the Hellenistic milieu in which everybody in the ancient Near East lived at the time. Philosophy demanded a hearing equal to that accorded revelation, among many educated Christians in that time and place—a more serious one, for some of them, and often little love was lost between the two. *What has Athens to do with Jerusalem?* Tertullian asked sourly late in the second century:

> What concord is there between the Academy and the Church? What between heretics and Christians? Our instruction comes from "the porch of Solomon," who had himself taught that "the Lord should be sought in simplicity of heart." Away with all attempts to produce a mottled Christianity of Stoic, Platonic, and dialectic composition! We want no curious disputation after possessing Christ Jesus, no inquisition after enjoying the gospel! With our faith, we desire no further belief.[2]

He may have deplored the trend mingling Christian faith with philosophical worldviews, but it was irresistible. Tertullian was part of it himself, spilling a fair amount of ink on philosophical treatises. His is the first formulation of the Trinity extant. His use of the word *trinity* is the oldest instance of it we have.

---

2 Tertullian, "De praescriptione haereticorum (On the prescription of heretics)," Chapter VII in The Ante-Nicene Fathers, ca. 208 ce, trans. Philip Holmes (1870).

Their project of making philosophical sense of Christ was very like ours, when we venture into discussions of faith and science. Wishing prematurely to pit one against the other and declare a winner, we miss the opportunity to allow them dialogue with each other. But the Bible managed in the end to be nourished in the church by both philosophy and revelation. Science and religion can and do synthesize in the same way.

A conversation:

> *In the beginning, there is no beginning. That it was a long time ago is for your convenience, not mine—I don't need beginnings and endings.*

Sorry?

> *Let me rephrase. In the beginning, there is one thing.*

But wait—look how many of us there are!

> *There is one thing.*

But look how many planets, how many white-tailed deer and asteroids, look how many rocks there are, and how much water! What do you mean, there is one thing?

> *There is the fact of existence. There is nothing else. Everything you have named comes from it.*

What's the point of it, then?

> *It needs no "point," except that it is its nature to exist.*

Where do the white-tailed deer come from, then, and all the rocks?

> *Existence is energy. An explosion of being is its expression.*

Why does "one thing" need expression? To whom does it express?

It doesn't need expression. But you need a beginning. So existence explodes into motion. On and on it courses through the emptiness, creating directions as it goes. Faster and faster it goes, and as it goes, it creates its own path of being.

Wait, how do we know this happened?

Happens, please. You don't know. It could just as easily not happen. But you are here, so clearly something has happened. Let there be light, you know?

Oh, jeez. Go on.

Existence in motion includes all things, from neutrinos to protozoa to the sperm whale to the planet Jupiter. Suns and planets form and find location. Our sun is one of them, and our earth.

There can be water and rocks, and so there are. Chemicals combine and react with one another. Here and there, a promising protein soup forms—maybe a million of them. And in one, just the right combination becomes organic—so basic a being that it is premature to ask if it is plant or animal. But it is alive. Soon there are more. They live in the water. The energy of their creation continues to explode, and the simple beings differentiate—now we can discuss leaves, roots, brains, gills. One of them crawls up onto a rock that protrudes above the surface, but can't take it and slides back into the water. More try and fail—many die trying. But then one makes it, and stays. Pretty soon we're talking fur and legs. In no time, it's campfires and cities, gold amulets and steam engines and atom smashers.

And that's not a lot of things?

Oh, it is. But they are also all part of the one thing. The explosion of energy. Different aspects, of it, you might say. Different forms.

Me and an amoeba? Different forms of the same thing?

Sure. Why not?

How about me and a rock?

Why not? You think a rock is inert because it looks motionless to you. But it teems with molecular motion. The distinction between organic and inorganic seems huge to you. It doesn't to me, though.

Is this a conversation that could not have taken place before we had relativity and quantum physics? No, it's an ancient conversation. The theologians of the early church had the same conversation among themselves, as they struggled to combine a faith rooted in the concrete and very relational world of the Hebrew Scriptures with the coolness of the Greek philosophy that was the intellectual environment of their day. The historic creeds they authored together, arguing fiercely every step along the way, are succinct accounts of the struggle to have the Incarnation make sense: to fit the man Jesus, whose history was receding further and further into the past, into an increasingly sophisticated philosophical matrix. This was a formidable task, and they did the best they could. That we continue to recite the creeds today is more an homage to their place in our tradition than a sign of our intellectual assent to their contents. "God from God, light from light, true God from true God, begotten, not made," was once an intelligible and living statement. Certainly it is possible to *explain* this and other phrases like it to a modern person, but nobody could say—even after having done so—that it carries deep and clear spiritual resonance to modern ears.

What we *can* say is that considering the presence of God in our experience is an ancient part of what it has always meant to be a person of faith. Using the best tools available to them in the best way they know, theologians have always brought fresh eyes to bear on ancient words. So it is with us, when we look at the sacred texts of our forebears—we cannot un-know what we now know. We must not put our words in their mouths, but we can find hints in what they have left us, points of contact between our experience and theirs.

So when Jesus speaks of the kingdom of heaven as a current reality, rather than a future event, we who have just finished throwing cold water on the time line we used in grammar school sit up and take notice. Hmmm . . . . Not a place, heaven. Not a time, either—the notion of the righteous dead lying still in their coffins, patiently waiting until a general resurrection at the end of the line, becomes unnecessary if there is no *duration*. If everything is now. There is no need to wait, for the kingdom of heaven is now, just as surely as it is to come or, as we say in church, "as it was in the beginning, is now, and ever shall be." Just as the multiplicity of creation is also the singularity—all the animals, plants, rocks, everything, expressions of the singular fact of existence—so the times are one, as well. Past, present, future—one time.

I think of a film that shows in moving images what God's timelessness and spacelessness might mean to us. It is "Dead Man Walking"—specifically, the execution scene at the end. As you may recall, the protagonist is a young man who has participated in the brutal murder of two teenagers. He is a completely unsympathetic character: a violent white supremacist punk whose life has been a series of failures to be accountable for his own actions. He has been convicted of the murders, and sentenced to die by lethal injection. His conviction and sentencing inaugurate a long legal process of appeals, which takes years to unfold. Throughout this time he is accompanied by Sr. Helen Prejean, C.S.J., whose fight to save his life forms the story line of the book upon which the film is based.

Sr. Helen's tireless advocacy of the convicted man over years is not without cost. Very few in her world understand her commitment; most find it amoral. Why stand with such a manifestly unrepentant criminal, especially when it is clear that her effort will be to no avail? In the end, all appeals exhausted, no pardon on its way from the governor, the execution will go forward. The families of the dead teenagers are there, watching through a heavy plate glass window. The press is there. The man's attorney is there. The condemned is strapped, cruciform, to a gurney, with an IV drip in each arm. One of them will introduce a harmless saline solution into his bloodstream, while the other will deliver the poison that will take his life. No one will know which was which. The signal is given, and the twin drips begin.

Here is where the film does what no book can ever do: the camera begins to pan around the scene, and we go with it. We see the man as death starts to steal into his body. We see the warden. We see Sister Helen and the lawyer. We see the parents of the dead teenagers. We see the man, the parents, the man, the warden, the sister, the man, the warden, the parents, the man, the parents, the man, warden, the sister, around and around we go and then—then we see the victims alive, standing still, looking calmly at us, clean, uninjured, not even a wrinkle in their clothing. And then again, the man, the sister, the warden, the man, the parents and then—the two victims again, calm, clean, unafraid, and unhurt. Then we see the murder itself—terrible, chaotic. Still the camera moves: again and again we see everything, one thing yielding to another. We see it all at the same time.

This is how God sees history. We must stretch it out in a line order to encompass it. God doesn't have to do that.

Humankind cannot bear very much reality. Here in this life we cannot see things as they are. We see only a portion of what they are. For as long as we live here, this is how it is with us.

But within our tradition and also within our experience, there are traces of this larger vision, glimpses of the existence that contains our own existence. I've mentioned a few that everybody knows about, like déjà vu and the elasticity of time in our dreams. The frequent use of a present tense in Jesus's metaphors about the kingdom of heaven. The relativity of time observed in space travel, and the manner in which the vast distances in the universe permit us to behold the past in our present. We know a bit about these things from our experience. But they live in our tradition, too: slivers of timelessness.

CHAPTER 4

THE HARROWING OF HELL

When I was a girl, we recited the Apostles' Creed in church every Sunday—not the Nicene, as ours was a parish in which Morning Prayer was the principal service most Sundays, rather than the Eucharist. This was before the middle-aged volume some old-timers still call the New Prayer Book came out, so our creed was in the Elizabethan prose in which all Episcopal worship was conducted in those days.

There were many advantages to an Episcopal childhood. It endowed us with lots of special words, words like "propitiation" and "inestimable" and "schism," words that our schoolmates didn't know and about which I remember being rather vain. Our familiarity with the cadence of sixteenth-century speech made Shakespeare a snap when the time came to study it in school. We felt we had the best of several worlds: none of the tiresome fasts our Roman Catholic classmates had to observe, nor the social interdiction of things like dancing, as our Protestant chums endured. There was not much in the way of attempts to manage our behavior through guilt. Common sense and common courtesy provided a sufficient rubric for our moral education.

Still, we were not immune to the thrill of a little skate on thin moral ice when we could find some, and the Apostles' Creed afforded us an opportunity to do just that every Sunday. Specifically, it contained the phrase "He descended into Hell." We were not permitted to say words like "hell" and "damn." That was swearing. But here was a cuss word right there in the prayer book! We could hardly believe our good fortune. In the 1928 book we used, there was an option for people with delicate sensibilities to substitute "the place of departed spirits" for "Hell," but we didn't do that in my church, nor did I know of any other church that did. Nope, we called a spade a spade in our church, and every week we marched straight ahead and sang it out. "He descended into Hell" we'd say, and kids would steal delighted glances at each other behind the devout backs of our parents.

I used to wonder what this was all about. I asked my grandmother once and got what I thought was an evasive answer. If we had lived in an earlier century, she would have set more store by the tradition that Jesus went to hell after his burial to retrieve the righteous dead, whose only crime was having been born before he was, and who had waited patiently for centuries for him to appear, grow to adulthood, and destroy the power of death by dying himself. The harrowing of hell would not have been the antiquarian curiosity it has become in our age.

More than mere squeamishness about swearing in church lay behind the rubric suggesting an alternative to the word "Hell" that I remember from the prayer book of my childhood. The harrowing of hell was an ambiguous idea from the beginning—it didn't have much in the way of Scripture to back it up, and it collided with the complicated calculus of reward and punishment that grew more and more intricate as the Christian centuries passed. The more horrendous hell became in art and letters, the harder it was to imagine Christ going there. Theologians were at considerable pains to be sure we understood that it was only to retrieve the *righteous* dead that he made that journey—the damned were staying right where they were. They were needed—the terrible warning they telegraphed from the cathedral frescoes and stone friezes kept sinners in mind of their continual need for the absolution that only the church could offer. The Jewish *Sheol* had been a more or less neutral place where the dead went: avoiding it had never been a central motivating factor for peoples' good behavior on earth. But now the stakes were higher, both for the church and for the individual Christian: All manner of ways by which eternal punishment might be mitigated or even avoided altogether presented themselves, and some of them involved real money. Hell needed to be excruciatingly actual and permanent, if wealthy sinners were to be motivated to avoid it, and guilt was the necessary lubricant of this very profitable mechanism. The divine compassion needed to stay within fiscal boundaries—why would anyone wish to buy what Christ was giving away for free? A Holy Saturday visit from the Savior fit poorly into a Western church whose principal iconographic expression of faith became the crucifixion. Though there are many iconic representations of the harrowing of hell from the early Christian centuries, few representations of the crucifixion in the West date from the church's first thousand years. After then, the harrowing of hell thins out quite a bit, while the crucifix is everywhere.

The Harrowing of Hell[1]

Hmmm. Although the oldest gospel accounts are about the passion and death of Jesus, the oldest Christian art isn't. Most of it is about the victory over death. And then, as time passes, the two change places. The Incarnation becomes a drama about Christ's battle against the earthly sins of individuals. The first Christians felt powerfully that they had been transformed. At first, many of them thought that they themselves would not see death at all. As time went by, this would prove not to be

1 From the Winchester Psalter, English, twelfth century. Now at the British Museum, Cotton MS. Nero C.iv.

the case. But they did not lose heart—in the pages of the New Testament, we hear them counseling one another not to fear the death of the body, not to shrink from the violent death that they knew some among them would endure. Jesus has trampled down death under his feet. The day-to-day tally of individual sins and their penalties, paid by a scapegoat Savior who would earn our way into heaven for us, grows in importance later on.

What would it cost us to revisit the harrowing of hell? To consider Christ's redeeming visit to the underworld without the belief that linear time is determinative of everything? To allow the mythic power of this ancient idea to remain mythic, not to try to force it into our age's narrow vision of what truth is? Or, to put it another way, to allow its most important truth to be not whether or not it happened, but what it meant?

Well, we would have to give up the medieval notion of heaven and hell.

We would have to give up fear of punishment as the primary reason for moral behavior.

We would have to enlarge the scope of our concern to include the whole of creation, not just our own individual dramas.

And we would have to give up our assumption that the only things that can happen in the universe are the things that can happen here on earth.

I've said that many Christians would sooner do without heaven than without hell. This was only partially a joke: We seek to baptize our own vindictiveness. We hope and believe that God dislikes the same things we dislike. Our history tells a sorry tale of what we have been willing to do in the service of this conviction—I doubt if any one group has killed more fellow human beings out of a conviction that they were an abomination in the sight of God than Christians have. But there is more to our devotion to the idea of hell than a shallow parochialism. We have another, more defensible reason for our consistent belief in a punitive afterlife: our longing for justice.

We long for a higher court than the one we so often encounter here, where the innocent suffer and the guilty prosper. Life is so unfair, we tell each other when we read of yet another tragic example in the newspaper, and we want life to be fair. Where's the justice in that, we demand, when yet another atrocity comes along.

We have inherited our idea of justice as fairness. We've even inherited its allegorical representation: a blindfolded woman who holds a scale in one upraised hand. She symbolizes the Western legal profession. She appears—or at least her balanced scale does—carved permanently into the stone facades of our courthouses. We want the scale to balance, for the rights of all to be accorded equal weight. We want all of life to be like that, not just the law. We do not want our sorrows to outweigh our joys.

But don't we actually want more? Think of that image for a moment, the blind woman holding a scale. We do not inherit her from the Hebrew scriptures; she is not a Judeo-Christian figure. Jesus does not allude to her—in his parable of the vineyard, for instance, he specifically rejects our symmetrical idea of fairness. One group of laborers begins work at dawn, and expects to receive more than the group who didn't start until it was almost quitting time. But no: both groups receive the same amount of money. Where's the fairness in *that*? No, the lady Justice is not from the Bible: she comes to us from the Greco-Roman world, and she symbolizes the mutual restraint of evil: *I will not injure you one bit more than you have injured me. If I do, we will agree upon a penalty, and I will pay it. Then we will be even.*

The balance of a scale like the one Justice holds is precarious. Load each side equally and you do have balance, but the scale trembles slightly, does it not? Stand on the scale at the doctor's office and carefully slide the weight across the bar until you arrive at your own weight. Again and again, the bar lands with a clunk; then, when you get it right, it hangs suspended. But doesn't the arrow tremble slightly, even when you have balanced the scale? It is balanced, but it is not stable. The balance of good and evil is precarious. It is not sturdy. It doesn't take much to tip it one way or the other.

Heaven and hell as we have developed them belong to the lady with the scale. But the divine justice of our ancient tradition is not about her—it is much more than the mutual restraint of evil a balanced scale represents. God's justice is not balance—it is righteousness. It is not blind. It is not neutral. It is active and in motion. It is not precarious. God's justice encounters a hard world and enters it powerfully on behalf of the weak.

A childless woman becomes a mother. Several do, in fact. It was a favorite theme.

The enslaved people of Israel escape a despotic king.

A young boy with a slingshot defeats a giant in full battle dress.

A prostitute saves her people from an invading army.

An unmarried girl, certain to face criticism and even physical danger because of her pregnancy, sees freedom from oppression and want in her situation, and sings a song of triumph about it.

A sworn enemy of the nascent church becomes its most eloquent preacher.

And, of course, a man who has died a criminal's death rises from the tomb.

This is the paradoxical vision of Scripture, more consistent than any other theme across the many centuries, cultures, and linguistic groups of its composition. That the world has never reflected the divine justice fully has never prevented us from imagining it, and its graceful presence can be seen in the midst of every era's sins and sorrows. It is the righteous Gentile in wartime France passing off a Jewish child as one of her own. It is the doctor son of a wealthy German spending his entire career serving the desperately poor in Africa. It is the mothers of the "disappeared" bringing down a military dictatorship, and Irish mothers demanding an end to bloodshed and getting it. It is a man imprisoned for twenty-seven years walking out into the sunshine with forgiveness in his heart. The divine justice is as big as the universe, but it is built bit by tiny bit. The divine justice is not primarily about punishing sin and violence. It is about ending it.

A hell like Dante's organizes and codifies the sorry parade of human sin. The vagueness of his heaven in comparison with his hell is telling—hell is where the real interest lies. Perhaps the harrowing of hell holds out a radical vision of what Christ means to humanity—Christ is better than our very worst. His goodness is more potent than our most potent evil. Sin and death are simply no match for him.

What might this mean to us? Down he goes after he dies, deep into the bowels of the earth, where the departed sleep. Up they all come, one by one, as he undoes the limitations of their human lives, limitations of time and space and circumstance. There are ancient Adam and ancient Eve, wrinkled and clothed in the aprons they stitched together to hide the sudden shame of their nakedness. There is David, crowned and holding his harp, so we will recognize him, and there is Moses, with his ambiguous horns. Prophets, patriarchs, kings and queens, nameless common folk. Fewer and fewer remain below, one might suppose, until at last hell is empty.

Wait—what?!? It didn't take long for the church to shrink from *that* thought and to attach strings to it. Oh no, we didn't mean *unrighteous* dead—just the good ones. But I wonder: how does that limitation comport with the transforming power of the creator? That some of us—that *any* of us—should be permanently beyond the reach of God's love? Is that not a modest view of a God with whom, as Mary observed, all things are possible? Perhaps we do not think all things are possible with God. Perhaps we have developed a commitment to hell as eternal punishment simply because we cannot imagine God doing things we are unable to do, cannot imagine anything beyond what we see and know. Can't imagine a God who could transform us after this earthly run is finished.

In this immense cosmos, how likely is it that we have only this short span of time—a hundred years or less—to determine the whole? How likely is it that what we see here is all there is? We can be forgiven for thinking at first that it might be, just as the Ptolemaic universe, with the Earth at its center, made sense when one simply looked up at the sky and saw that the planets move across it. But there were too many anomalies in a universe of which we were the center, we or our Earth or even our enormous sun, which we now know not to be enormous at all, as suns go. We had to move on from that, and the world made more sense when we did. In an analogous way, we are moving on from our captivity in time. We have hints of the kingdom of heaven, and it feels to us like something that does not yet exist. Something we will have to wait for, and wait a long, long time.

But remember—there can be no time in the kingdom of heaven. Time is *not* a line with an arrow pointing out into infinity, a line that stretches on and on and on. If it were, there would have to be a time before and a time after God. God's own self would have to be on that line. No: God holds all time, but time does not hold God. A number of things will make more sense to us if we can come to embrace the notion that there is no *duration*. There are only moments. And, in the kingdom of heaven, they are simultaneous. Everything that was, is. Everything that will be, is.

You are there.

Your injury is also there.

The moment before you were injured is there, and the moment before that.

The moment afterward is there, and your eventual healing from your injury.

All your moments are there, but you are trapped in none of them.

They are all now.

Your beloved is there.

The moment he died is there.

The moment before he died is there, and the moment after.

So is the year after. Ten years after.

And so is the moment you met.

The moment when he called and asked you to have dinner and a movie with him.

The day of your wedding is there.

The day you were so angry at him you told him you never wanted to see him again.

The day you changed your mind about that.

The whole of your life together is there.

They are all now.

Your matriculation is there. And your first semester.

You are there, thinking that seminary would take a long time.

Your graduation is there: you, wondering where the time went.

Your first church is there.

You are there, not even thinking about retirement yet.

You are there thirty-five years later, wondering how it can have been thirty-five years.

From lightning and tempest, from plague, pestilence, and famine, from battle and murder, and from sudden death, Good Lord, deliver us. The Book of Common Prayer lists human sins and sorrows with grim authority—the age of its composition was a violent one. Whether another person was the aggressor or merely indifferent nature, everyone felt their vulnerability, more than modern people allow ourselves to know of our own. Centuries later, we have cushioned ourselves from some of their dangers. But we have invented new ones to replace them: a world without enough water in it, a poisoned world, a world capable of destroying itself—these were not things they imagined, but we live every day with the specter of them at the dread periphery of our vision.

The enormity of the offense our losses give us is dependent upon our perception of linear time. Things hurt us all the more because they are irrevocable. Here is Lear, stumbling onstage with the lifeless body of his daughter in his arms:

> No, no, no life?
> Why should a dog, a horse, a rat, have life,
> And thou no breath at all? Thou'lt come no more,
> Never, never, never, never, never.[2]

Never, never, never, never, never—it *is* like five nevers when someone leaves us. Before it happens it seems impossible that the world could continue without her. The years of bereavement stretch endlessly out before you. *How will I endure this,* you ask yourself, and it seems that you will not. That his death is only a moment in the timelessness of his life in Christ may be true, but that is not how it seems to those of us who remain behind. One day will follow another, and another. Your days on earth will go on and on, and she's not going to be in any of them. In bereavement, there is no time off for good behavior.

2 King Lear, 5.3.369–372.

We want to undo this.

When we were children, we thought we could prevent sorrow by being good. Adults who were trying to make us behave ourselves promised to reward our virtues and punish our sins, and we learned to believe them. Naturally we assumed that God, whom we frequently heard described in parental language, managed things in the same way. Good behavior would produce enjoyable results, and its opposite would do the reverse.

One doesn't have to get very old, though, to begin noticing that this is not always the case. Whatever God is doing, it is not managing this neat symmetry. For a time, we rack our brains to try and make the model work. *Surely there's something I did to deserve this*, we say to ourselves as we lie in a hospital bed, but we come up empty. No, we were not perfect. But there were many more conspicuous sinners than we were who did not get our cancer, our Ebola, who did not end up paraplegic from a car crash as we did.

We didn't really believe Jesus when he said that the sun shines on the just as well as on the unjust, I guess. But he was simply describing an eminently discernible fact: life is unfair.

Our notion of reward and punishment is hard to surrender. Life would be so much clearer if it were steadily true! We stay with it for as long as we can, and are willing to alter biblical narratives to make them fit it if we have to.

The happy ending to Mark, the oldest gospel we have, *wasn't* in the story people told each other before it was written down. Here is how Mark ends in the earliest manuscripts we have in which the women are addressed by "a young man."

> "Do not be alarmed. You seek Jesus of Nazareth, who was crucified. He has risen; he is not here. See the place where they laid him. But go, tell his

> disciples and Peter that he is going before you to Galilee. There you will see him, just as he told you." And they went out and fled from the tomb, for trembling and astonishment had seized them, and they said nothing.[3]

That's all Mark wrote originally, most scholars think. No post-resurrection appearances at all. I recall being shocked when I first heard about this—in the Bible I grew up with, there were a dozen more very busy verses at the end of Mark, in which Jesus appeared, gave instructions, travelled, foretold the future, and then ascended. Still, it was true that these events were jumbled together in these verses, as if a writer had cobbled them together. And the Greek was different from that in the rest of Mark, though I would have had no inkling of *that* fact when I was a girl. Hmmm . . . and those stitched-together verses are not present in the oldest manuscripts.

Was a later scribe offended by the abruptness at the end of the gospel of Mark? Did he gather what he knew from other gospels and insert them, to preserve the idea that a concretely physical reward followed immediately from Jesus's radical obedience to God? That the Resurrection was more resuscitation than transformation? Most scholars think so.

What might it mean to us to consider the possibility that fidelity to God is not an algorithm by which we can earn—or escape—our just deserts. Would our behavior change if we no longer thought we would be either rewarded or punished for it? I suppose we must first ask ourselves how well this belief of ours has served us thus far. Has our venerable fear of hellfire made us good? How about our hope of heaven? The hope of heaven has long since been so intertwined with the fear of hell that the church has counted beholding the tortures of the

---

3 Mark 16:6–8.

damned among the pleasures of the righteous in heaven. Here is Thomas Aquinas's picture of this:

> Nothing should be denied the blessed that belongs to the perfection of their beatitude. . . . wherefore in order that the happiness of the saints may be more delightful to them and that they may render more copious thanks to God for it, they are allowed to see perfectly the sufferings of the damned.[4]

This harsh vision of blessedness did not die with the Middle Ages. It has survived through the centuries to this day. Here is Martin Luther in the sixteenth century:

> [God] When questioned whether the Blessed will not be saddened by seeing their nearest and dearest tortured answers, "Not in the least."

And the revivalist preacher Jonathan Edwards in the seventeenth century:

> Today God stands ready to pity you. This is a day of mercy. You may cry now with some hope of receiving mercy. But once the day of mercy is past, your most lamentable and mournful cries and shrieks will be in vain. You will be forever lost and thrown away by God with no regard for your welfare. God will have no other use for you than to serve as a vessel for his wrath. He will be so far from pitying you that when you cry to him, he will only laugh and mock you as it says in Proverbs 1:26.

Scottish Calvinist preacher and theologian Thomas Boston in the eighteenth century:

4 *Summa Theologica, Supplementum Tertia Partis,* Question 94, Article 1.10.

> God shall not pity them, but laugh at their calamity. The righteous company in heaven shall rejoice in the execution of God's judgement, and shall sing while the smoke riseth up for ever.

And in *The Sight of Hell*, a book for children written in the mid-nineteenth century by the aptly-named John Furniss:

> The little child is in the red hot oven. Hear how it screams to come out; see how it turns and twists itself about in the fire. It beats its head against the roof of the oven. It stamps its little feet on the floor.

This book was not an outlier. It sold four million copies. It is still in print in several editions (you can get it in a Kindle version), and it's doing better on Amazon than some of my books. Still, a welcome failure of nerve where hell is concerned has overtaken many Christian writers and teachers in recent decades. Here is the vicar general of Dublin's informal *nihil obstat* prefacing the 1855 first edition of *The Sight of Hell:*

> I have carefully read over this Little Volume for Children and have found nothing whatsoever in it contrary to the doctrine of Holy Faith; but, on the contrary, a great deal to charm, instruct and edify our youthful classes, for whose benefit it has been written.[5]

Contrast the vicar general's compliments with the genuine alarm shown 150 years later in the publisher's warning to parents on the title page of the 2000 edition. It quotes the earlier compliment in apparent disbelief:

5 John Furniss, *The Sight of Hell* (1855; Dublin: James Duffy and Co., Ltd., 1874), XXVIII, The Fifth Dungeon, 28.

> This book, although written to "charm, instruct and edify youthful classes" in 1855, may be too graphic or frightening for today's young children of the third millennium. Parental discretion is strongly advised.

That being the case, one might question the decision to bring *The Sight of Hell* out again for the twenty-first century. It can only be because the publisher thought it would sell. The worldview it represents survives and thrives today in many places, Catholic and Protestant—most recently in the conspicuous preaching of the Westboro Baptist Church, the church frequently in the news picketing funerals of American service personnel because the armed services no longer ban LGBT persons from serving in the military.

> Q. Why do you preach hate?
>
> A. Because the Bible preaches hate. For every one verse about God's mercy, love, compassion, etc., there are two verses about His vengeance, hatred, wrath, etc. The maudlin, kissy-pooh, feel-good, touchy-feely preachers of today's society are damning this nation and this world to hell. They are telling you what you want to hear rather than what you need to hear, just like what happened in the days of Isaiah and Jeremiah. . . . What you need to hear is that God hates people, and that your chances of going to heaven are nonexistent, unless you repent. What you need to hear is a little fire and brimstone preaching, like Jesus preached. What you don't need to hear is that you're okay just the way you are, and God accepts everyone without exception. Don't listen to the

> money-grubbing heretic who stands at the front of your church. Listen to God. If you are one of His elect, you'll hear. [6]

So we in heaven will delight in the torment of the ones who didn't make it?!? And God will do the same? That bespeaks a level of moral development somewhat south of the level I myself have reached already, and I am definitely a work in progress. God is far from finished with my formation, and yet even *I* know better than *that*. Of what does the thousand biblical years of which we have record tell us, if not of God's passionate desire for us to walk in righteousness and live? And of the divine willingness to assist us as we struggle to do that? One of my earliest memories in church is of this deeply comforting Absolution of Sin from the Episcopal Church's 1928 Prayer Book, which quoted the prophet Ezekiel (33:1). I had not the slightest doubt that it applied to me:

> Almighty God, the Father of our Lord Jesus Christ, who desireth not the death of a sinner, but rather that he may turn from his wickedness and live, hath given power, and commandment, to his Ministers, to declare and pronounce to his people, being penitent, the Absolution and Remission of their sins. He pardoneth and absolveth all those who truly repent, and unfeignedly believe his holy Gospel.
>
> Wherefore let us beseech him to grant us true repentance, and his Holy Spirit, that those things may please him which we do at this present; and that the rest of our life hereafter may be pure and holy; so that at the last we may come to his eternal joy; through Jesus Christ our Lord. Amen.

6 From the website of the Westboro Baptist Church, www.godhatesfags.com, under "Frequently Asked Questions."

I had no acquaintance with a God who was disposed to punish me or anyone else with eternal fire. Our focus was never on punishment—it was on amendment of life. How might I do better next time? I didn't know how fortunate I was in this formation until I began to visit the churches my school friends attended, some of which emphasized salvation in a way that made me wonder how free a gift grace really was there.

So I guess the harrowing of hell was a success, as far as I was concerned, even before I knew what it was. There was no need to live in terror of a God who loved us. There was no depth to which we could sink from which Christ was unwilling to redeem us. And there was more than one chance—Jesus would save me as often as I needed saving.

But not from misfortune. A portion of that would fall to me, as it falls to everyone. We are not saved from the earthly consequences of earthly actions. We are not saved from freak accidents. What we are saved from is a life unaware of who we are: the children of God in the image of God. We are saved, and the world is also saved, from joyless replication of the harshness of so punitive a God as the one so many have imagined for centuries and continue to imagine today. Nobody is permanently free from sorrow. But we can be free from wrath.

At the beginning of Nathaniel Hawthorne's *The Scarlet Letter*, Hester Prynne steps forth from the Salem jailhouse in which she has been confined for the crime of adultery. She carries her infant daughter, evidence of her illicit affair, and wears a scarlet letter *A* on the bodice of her gown as a token of her shame. The letter is part of her sentence; she must wear it for the rest of her life. An eager crowd of villagers gathers.

> "What do we talk of marks and brands, whether on the bodice of her gown or the flesh of her forehead?" cried another female, the ugliest as well as

> the most pitiless of these self-constituted judges. "This woman has brought shame upon us all, and ought to die; is there not law for it? Truly there is, both in the Scripture and the statute-book. Then let the magistrates, who have made it of no effect, thank themselves if their own wives and daughters go astray."
>
> "Mercy on us, goodwife!" exclaimed a man in the crowd, "is there no virtue in woman, save what springs from a wholesome fear of the gallows?"

That's a good question: if there's not going to be a direct reward for virtue or punishment for sin, why bother being good?

Many have asked it. And the man in the crowd in this story seems to have thought there was a reason for goodness apart from fear, or he would not have reproved the woman who called for Hester's death.

Plato told a story of a man named Gyges who found a magic ring that gave him the power to become invisible. He murdered the king, married the queen and became king himself, and nobody was any the wiser because nobody saw him commit his crimes. Obviously Gyges was an egoist. Since he was an egoist, was there any reason—that would matter to him—not to have behaved as he did? Socrates thought Gyges's behavior wouldn't really be in his own interest, even if that were the only good he recognized, that he wouldn't be really happy—he would be what we today would call psychologically damaged. But it's hard to imagine a psychopath like Gyges recognizing that fact about himself, or giving it any weight if he did.

Augustine of Hippo was a realist, with a deep appreciation for the ambiguity of human nature and plenty of hands-on experience of just what it was like to be tempted. He had a pessimistic view of our capacity to act from a sense of duty alone: *If you cannot love what he promises, at least fear what he threatens*, he wrote, but he held out scant hope that we would do either of these very well or for very long. *Who can embrace wholeheartedly that which gives him no delight?* Nobody, that's who, was his answer. He went on. *But who can determine for himself that what will delight him should come his way and that, when it comes, it will, in fact, delight him? (Ad Simpl I, ii, 22).*

The eighteenth-century Scottish philosopher David Hume recast the Gyges story in his *Enquiry Concerning the Principals of Morals*, introducing the figure of the Sensible Knave. Like Gyges, the knave is amoral. He behaves ethically when it suits his ends, but feels no compunction about sinning when it does not. His actions are never in the service of an ideal other than self-interest. He is "sensible" because he is capable of restraining his desires when giving them free rein would injure him, but has no personal commitment to the well-being of others if their well-being is not instrumental to his own. Is there a reason why he should behave himself? On his own terms, there is not. Only the scheme of reward and punishment, heaven and hell—in which Hume seems to put little stock—could limit him. As for the Socratic conviction that only a life of virtue can be a truly happy life, Hume gives lip service to it,

> Inward peace of mind, consciousness of integrity . . . these are very requisite to happiness . . . knaves . . . have sacrificed the invaluable enjoyment of a character for the acquisition of worthless toys.

but acknowledges that the knave considers himself well enough supplied with happiness already, and is unlikely to go in pursuit of deeper enjoyment.

Our bloodthirsty commitment to the existence of hell

comports well with the notion of a vengeful God. But the idea of hell has performed another function: it has embodied the human longing for justice to be restored. When the weak suffer at the hands of the cruel and powerful, they are apt to live and die without ever seeing the tables turned. Their tormentors live and die without ever paying for their misdeeds. The scales of justice are tipped in favor of the mighty much more often than they are balanced. We know this, and it offends us. We know that we cannot restore to the victims of human cruelty what has been taken from them. The ending of Job, in which he gets a new house, new animals, new, prettier daughters after the first batch has been destroyed, is cartoonish, precisely because we know this not to be the way the world works. We are *not* neatly reimbursed for everything we lose. Our losses are resounding and permanent.

Here is where, sometimes, the God who desireth not the death of a sinner fails to satisfy us. We cannot help but hear the innocent's cry, which an indifferent universe seems not to hear. The wrong done here is allowed to stand, and the perpetrator walks away. We won't stand for this; we want her avenged. We want blindfolded Justice to hurry back to us, so we can balance her tilted scale. At these times, it is not just God who is offended. We are offended, too, and long to punish. It seems to us that the dead are soothed by the suffering of their murderers. If God does not prevent the suffering of the innocent, we say, then at least those guilty of causing it can suffer too, and rightly.

In Western literature, there is no more famous articulation of this demand than that of the bitter Ivan in Dostoevsky's *The Brothers Karamazov.* He confronts his brother Alyosha, a novice monk, with three terrible examples of cruelty to children. A girl of seven is beaten by her father so hard and for so long that at length she cannot speak, until she can only gasp

"Daddy! Daddy!" A little boy who accidentally injured one of a rich man's hunting dogs slightly is set upon by all the dogs, and his mother forced to watch them tear him to pieces. A five-year-old girl is shut up in an outhouse all night in the depth of a Russian winter for soiling her bed linens. Here, he mocks the idea that reconciliation in heaven will put things right:

> I don't want the mother to embrace the oppressor who threw her son to the dogs! She dare not forgive him! Let her forgive him for herself, if she will, let her forgive the torturer for the immeasurable suffering of her mother's heart. But the sufferings of her tortured child she has no right to forgive; she dare not forgive the torturer, even if the child were to forgive him! And if that is so, if they dare not forgive, what becomes of harmony? Is there in the whole world a being who would have the right to forgive and could forgive? I don't want harmony. From love for humanity I don't want it. I would rather be left with the unavenged suffering.[7]

But the prospect of a symmetry of offense and punishment in hell brings Ivan no relief, either:

> It's not worth it, because those tears are unatoned for. They must be atoned for, or there can be no harmony. But how? Is it possible? By their being avenged? But what do I care for avenging them? What do I care for a hell for oppressors, since those children have already been tortured?[8]

In Ivan's righteous fury, the agony of *chronos* is clearly

7 F. Dostoevsky, *The Brothers Karamazov*, Part II, Book V: Pro and Contra, Chapter 4: Rebellion.

8 Ibid.

visible. In *chronos*, our lives are one unfulfilled longing for justice after another. Such balance as we find is always too little, too late—whatever retributive justice we can muster will not restore what has been lost. The moments of pain and despair simply cannot be balanced against a future happiness—even if a balance could be found, it would fail to satisfy.

> If the sufferings of children go to swell the sum of suffering which was necessary to pay for truth, then I protest that the truth is not worth such a price.[9]

Alyosha has been very quiet throughout this long conversation, only a fraction of which has been reproduced here. He makes no defense of God, nor any of what Ivan mockingly calls "harmony." Instead, he leans toward his brother and kisses him.

In what sense could a kiss answer such righteous anger? Certainly not in any logical sense. Certainly not with a superior argument, one that makes everything finally fall into place. The offense is not removed from history. What has happened has still happened. Things don't un-happen in *chronos*.

They don't un-happen in *kairos*, either: they happen at the same time. There is no injury separate from the wholeness of the moment before it happened. There is no before and no after. There is only now. Nobody must suffer for years or wait for decades—there is no elapse of time. Nobody waits for anything. There is no *duration*. There is no distance that must be traveled between this state and the next; we are already there. The *alsolife* is not endless *chronos*. But neither is the *alsolife* nirvana: it is not empty of everything. It is full of everything.

In the *alsolife*, nothing is lost.

9 Ibid.

CHAPTER 5

MEMENTO MORI

It means "remember that you will die."

The Black Death killed upwards of one-third to half of Europe in the fourteenth century. Its dreadful visitations combined with the carnage of the wars that raged throughout almost all of that century, and with the general hazards of medieval life, to produce a fatalism that permeated every level of society.

Most people who contracted the Black Death were gone within a week, some within a day. Entire families, entire neighborhoods, entire villages were depopulated. In some places there were too few of the healthy to care for the sick, and too few of the living to bury the dead, who were left in their infected houses to be food for rats—who would then fan out to find new homes, where their fleas would infect new victims. Nobody knew then that it was fleas that caused the disease. Science had yet to understand the nature of contagion; it was thought that the plague was caused by the evil alignment of certain stars, which caused an atmospheric condition called *miasma*—"bad air."[1]

Memento mori was already ancient by the time of the Black Death. Meditation upon one's own death was a favorite philosophical theme among the stoics, and Plato wrote in the *Phaedo* that philosophy was "about nothing else but dying and being dead"—a bit of an overstatement, perhaps, but this was in connection with the death of Socrates, so we can allow him some poetic license. The preacher of Ecclesiastes bases his dismissal of all earthly aspiration as "vanity" on the fact that it all ends in death—in his memory, some *memento mori* paintings are called "vanities."

Here is a very old mosaic on the theme, from the first century of the common era. It is unusual: the skeleton combined with the verbal warning was not common at this time, as it would become much later on. Nevertheless, it is here:

Unknown mosaic artist, "Know Thyself" Roman, 1st century. Excavations in the Convent of San Gregorio on the Via Appia.

1 For a compelling account of the devastating plague years in Europe, see Barbara Tuchman's 1978 study *A Distant Mirror: The Calamitous 14th Century*.

In this fifteenth-century French book of hours, Death leads a wealthy man away from his counting table.

The man looks back longingly at his money,

while this man asks to finish reading his book, to no avail.

Not even the abbot can talk his way out of death.

Cadaver tomb of Richard Fleming, Bishop of Lincoln, 1431

Memento mori. It was and remains everywhere in art and literature, theology, and music. Stone cadavers, naked or shrouded, stretched on their shelves beneath stone effigies of the departed as they were in life, fully clothed, plump, and serene on the tops of their fifteenth-century sarcophagi. Partially decomposed or completely skeletal, they adorned the tombs of the rich and famous, people whose earthly life was powerful and privileged, in hopes that we who remained would reflect upon the transitory nature of worldly glory.

In *memento mori* art, as shown on the following page, a skull is central, usually with an hourglass or a watch or a sputtering candle nearby, and perhaps a flower or a butterfly, indicating both the beauty and the fragile brevity of life.

Philippe de Champaigne, *Vanitas* (ca. 1671)

In works other than portrait or still life, the artists' moral imaginations and no small amount of humor have free rein. In some, Death lurks at dinner parties, either invisible to the diners or appearing suddenly, throwing everyone at the party into a panic.

Giovanni Martinelli, *Death Comes to the Dinner Table,* Italian, ca. 1640–45

The juxtaposition of youth, beauty, and death was a favorite theme, as was the "Dance of Death" (*Danse macabre)* in which the skeletons dance energetically, while their human partners drag their feet.

Vincent de Kastav, *The Dance of Death*, Croatian, 1474

In Hans Holbein the Younger's 1533 painting *The Ambassadors*, two worthies stand competently before us, the tools of the knowledge and power to which they have committed their lives surrounding them.

But notice the foreground: a phantom skull lies diagonally across the canvas. We can only see it if we look at the painting at a certain angle. Here it is, overleaf and to the right.

You do not know the day or the hour. In the midst of life, you are in death.

Memento mori.

In 2012, St. Paul's Cathedral in London unveiled a new statue of its most famous dean, the poet John Donne. It is outdoors, in a new garden to the south of the cathedral. It faces west, but Donne's face is turned to face east. This is meant to remind us of his famous poem "Good Friday, 1613, Riding Westward," and a couplet from the poem is inscribed beneath the bust.

Hence is't, that I am carried towards the West,
This day, when my Soul's form bends to the East.

The east is the place of resurrection, of life and love. It is where the sun rises. Centuries of tradition have identified Christ with this compass point—it is why the altar end of a church is always called the "east end," even if it's not in the east according to the compass. The west is the place of death and darkness.

There is much well placed in this new statue, as it contains and celebrates Donne's remarkable literary achievements, his fame as a preacher, his love of the city he surveys. It's a good one to place in a beautiful new cathedral garden. But it is not the only statue of the dean in St. Paul's. The other one, which Donne commissioned and *posed for*—getting up from his deathbed to do so—shows him in his winding sheet, arising from his own funerary urn. Certainly Donne was aware of his own importance in the world and in the church, but this was not what he wanted his statue to convey. What he wanted, and what he got, was a *memento mori.*

Visit St. Paul's and find the statue—it is just south of the choir. Scorch marks from the Great Fire of 1666 still mar the base. The fire destroyed most of London. This statue was the only cathedral artwork to survive it.

Look sharp, mortal! Anything can happen. *Memento mori.*

The *memento mori* tradition made its way across the sea into the New World in the form of the death's-head angels found in all cemeteries of the colonial period and well into the early nineteenth century. The death's-head angel allowed Protestants to memorialize their dead in art without resorting to the iconography they rejected as popish. By the late eighteenth century it could often stand alone, without the poetic warnings offered on older gravestones.

> Remember me as you pass by,
> As you are now, so once was I,
> As I am now, so you will be,
> Prepare for death and follow me.

And it became less skeletal—flesh covers most of the bones of the face in this eighteenth-century carving in Concord, Massachusetts. The death's-head angel is being replaced by what was called the "soul effigy"—less skeletal, less frightening, and much more abstract.

The further they got from the Puritan experience, the more cherubic and less fearsome the death's-head angels became. Gravestones were on their way to becoming the sentimental creations of the Victorian age, in which death would be euphemized as sleep and separated as far as possible from dread. In funerary art we see a movement away from a focus on decay and the fear of hell and toward a certain domestication of death, keeping the dead "in the family" by means of bonds of love that do not end when life ends.

For most people, the survival of familial love meant the continuation by remembrance of the physical body. The bereaved longed for the physical presence of the beloved dead. Of course they did—we do the same. With the invention of photography in the 1840s, a significant industry of post-mortem portraiture developed, leaving us images of the dead positioned amongst their living families in one last moment together. Photography was new and expensive. These were probably the only images, living or dead, families possessed of those they loved but would see no longer.

If these images are disconcerting, remember your own losses. Remember how you hungered for the smallest of souvenirs when someone you loved died, and it may make more sense. To have accepted the pain of dressing her in Sunday-best dress, of combing his hair, of arranging her in as lifelike a pose as possible, to have held the cold little hand and convinced the reluctant living child to do the same for a family portrait—they would not have undertaken such pain if they had not thought it important to do so, knowing that the next task would be to bury him.

In the photo at the left, look at the numb grief in the young father's face in the family group, his dead toddler on his knee. Note the schoolgirl's resistance as she turns her eyes as far away from her sister as she can.

Look at the little sister, her dead brother's hand on her shoulder, both of them dressed to the nines.

Look at the stair-step line of five siblings. The smaller boys are growing out of their jackets; their elder brother is growing into his. The little sister's blonde hair has been put in perfect sausage curls. Her eyes are closed; her little hands hang stiffly at her side. The big sister is now the only girl in the family. Henceforth, little sister will be only a memory.

The two sisters stand together in matching calico dresses. At first I thought only the younger one had died. Looking more closely, though, I see that there are two stands propping them in an upright position, one behind each girl. These were special equipment that the photographer kept just for memorial portraits. So maybe both sisters have died, at the same time and of the same illness. And in all these cases, death came suddenly—the dead children's faces and bodies are plump, not wasted. Until recently, they were in good health.

Memento mori.

Death is resounding to us. It is the central pain of *chronos*—in fact, it is the only one: Why would we mind the passing of time if it did not bring us closer to our final farewell?

Whatever its purpose has been throughout the ages—and it has had many purposes—*memento mori* is good advice now. As we ponder the possibilities of what the timelessness of God means for us, we do well not to cling so tightly to the life we know that we cannot experience the attraction of the life we do not yet know. This is why mystical theology has long made meditation upon one's own death a spiritual practice. It is why monks and nuns sometimes slept in their own coffins. We need to get used to the idea. Taking the time to think about my own death lessens my fear of it. It enables me to come to terms with the fact that dying is a normal part of life, that everyone who has ever lived has managed to do it and so will I. It helps me not to mistake temporary things for permanent ones, helps me hold what I have lightly.

Because none of us are getting out of here alive, and we take nothing with us when we leave.

There Is No Such Thing as Time

Moments in time have harassed
and haunted me throughout my life—
sad childhood days after my father's death,
the grievous loss of a son in premature labor,
the unexpected death of my best friend.
Living seemed only a prelude to dying.

But physics and Einstein made it all timeless
so that the spirit we know has endless life.
We will not observe a life alongside our own,
with no beginning and no ending, until we die.
Then the alsolife welcomes the afterlife—
not as what follows life's ending, but part of it.

So if there is no such thing as time
I want a new beginning that has no sadness
for the departed when their absence
on those special days has been so painful.
Bring me days when every chair at the table
is filled, and everyone is there.

—William Henry Langhorne
2011

CHAPTER 6

BUT HOW WILL I KNOW HER?

It was a conference for people whose children had died. You got a welcome packet when you registered, and a name tag to wear. Your tag had your name on it, and your child's name and age at the time of his death. It gave people a quick way to find others whose children might have died at more or less the same age.

We had preregistered, so ours were printed already when we got our packets. "Barbara Crafton," mine read, and then "David 0 Day."

David 0 Day.

I put it on, and took a turn around the room. There were a couple of thousand people there, every one of them for the same unthinkable reason. Lots of young children's names: Kristin 3 . . . Brian 2 . . . Jose 5. Lots of teenagers: Betsy 15 . . . Daniel 17 . . . Jackie 19 . . . There were older parents there, too, with children not much younger than I was myself. Michael 46 . . . Lynn 55 . . . Beth 37.

I was jealous of all of them.

There was a photo board, upon which you could post a picture of your child. Prom pictures, kindergarten graduation pictures, pictures under the Christmas tree, babies in blankets, kids on motorcycles. I had no picture. They didn't have ultrasound back then. David was much too small to be born. There were no pictures of David 0 Day.

That seemed small-minded of me, to feel jealous. Here was a fellowship of people who all had known unspeakable loss; there was no need to create a hierarchy of pain. *Get over yourself.* But the heart doesn't always make sense: I wanted to have held him in my arms, not just in the palm of my hand. I wanted a birthday picture. I wanted a little undershirt to keep, one that smelled like him. I wanted to know what he smelled like. But there was none of that.

Then I saw her—another woman with an 0 Day baby! A little girl, Molly. Molly 0 Day.

Molly O'Day. Sounds Irish, I told her with a grin. The O'Days.

She smiled, and we talked about not having any pictures and the jealousy of which we were ashamed. Or maybe we weren't. Well, maybe not all the time, anyway. I felt better after chatting with her. That's what the conference is for: there aren't many people you can talk to about losing a child after some time has passed. People move on, and you move on, too. But not from that. Not from that child who will be the same age forever. *Gosh,* someone says uncertainly when they hear about the conference, *is that wise? Wouldn't it just remind you?*

Remind me? *Remind* me? You mean in case it slipped my mind that my baby died? I don't need a reminder.

I felt good enough to be of some use to a woman who stumbled into the ladies' room in tears, the mother of a suicide to whom somebody had said something unthinkingly cruel about his having "brought it on himself." There would be a small group about that the next day, I told her as she pulled paper towels out of the dispenser to wipe her eyes. *They'll all be parents whose children have completed suicide,* I said, handing her a packet of tissues from my purse. *Go to it.*

We talked about her son and his depression, the way it had sucked the joy out of him. How he had tried and tried to be okay. About the tears that stood in his blue eyes when he couldn't. About the hospital. And the other hospital, and another one. About how his dad found him hanging in the attic stairwell, his body still warm. If only they hadn't stopped for gas on the way home, she said. Her eyes were blue, too, and tears stood in them.

Lord, have mercy.

I walked back to the hotel room. I had been of use to somebody. That was good—care for others had long been my drug of choice. I lay down on the bed. When I turned on my side, the name tag was still around my neck. David 0 Day. And a vision came to me, or something like a vision: a sunny playroom, where all the little O'Days played together. They were toddlers now. They were all dressed alike, in blue and white plaid rompers. My Davey painted at an easel with a little Japanese girl. He looked like my brother did when he was little. Others played with trucks on the floor. Some sat at a little table and colored. A few clustered around a toy kitchen. I close my eyes and I can see them at play there still, right now, as I write these words. Our little Irish children, my little Irish boy, the sister and brother O'Days, safe and happy and healthy and growing. I am not Irish. But my little boy is one of the O'Days.

How will I know her? Will he still know me?

A cell and another cell meet and combine. Immediately division and growth begins, and they seek a home in which to grow. They find one, a perfect nest in the uterine wall, and they settle in, now no longer two but one, and that one growing.

But sometimes they don't find a home, and perish without their mother ever knowing they were there.

Sometimes they do find a home but can't establish a secure attachment there. Again they perish, without anyone even knowing they were there.

Sometimes they find a home, attach and grow. A tiny heart begins to beat. Month gives way to month and now *everyone* knows they are there. A nursery is furnished, baby clothes laid in, diapers washed and folded and ready. A name is chosen. And then something happens, and now there is no tiny heartbeat. Maybe nobody ever knows why.

Usually, though, that is not what happens. Usually growth continues, and birth ushers the baby into life. Usually the universe opens hospitable arms to one more child, who grows up beloved and loves right back, for years and years. This is usually how it is. Throughout all these years, decades of them, love twines its way around the hearts of too many people ever to untangle. For better or for worse, they say one day, and love becomes indissoluble. New lives come among us, loved and longed for before they even appear.

And then it comes to an end.

Intellectually, we're fine with the notion that there is no such thing as time in the larger life. That past, present, and future are all one thing. That linear time is a feature of life on earth. Fine.

And that everything that composes us continues in other forms? Also fine.

That we will compost future generations, not just with the repurposing of our physical cells but with the energy of our thought and our love—fine. Happy to help.

But we want our separate personalities to remain. We want them to cruise on into the larger life intact, still separate, still recognizable, still ourselves. We want our beloved dead to become angels, looking just like they did here but with wings. Even the little ones like my little David, who never had a chance to get to know us—we want them to be as they would have been had they lived here. I want my fantasy of the sunny nursery in which they play to be a fact. I want to visit it someday.

How will I know him?

Can we still be said to exist if our separateness ends? If I am even now in Christ, and when I have died live fully in Christ and know it, am I then still myself? Have I not been joined with Christ and ceased to be me?

No, that's not how it is. It is our separateness that is the illusion. Nothing ceases to be in the *alsolife.* Every specific molecule, every pulse of energy that ever was will always have been, and all that has been IS. This pair of eyes cannot look upon my beloved in this moment, but that happy gaze abides in an existence which is never forced to surrender its moments to the past, as we must. God sees it all, and so do we in our resurrected state. Not so much here and now—only glimpses. But face-to-face one day, and that day is already today. We just don't know it.

Right after the death, the suffering is all you see. The hospital bed, the tubes, the weakness, the pallor, the smell. It takes a while for the pictures of happier days to return. But they do. At first, they taunt, but eventually they comfort. Gratitude for having had love at all takes its place beside outrage at having love snatched away. Whatever is true now, you learn to say, she will always have been. I had love. I *have* it, in fact—my love has not lessened with my loss. If anything, it has grown.

Sometimes, there are dreams in which they come to us. Not often—*not often enough*, you are apt to say wistfully, the dreams are such happy ones. Sometimes there are coincidences, odd things that only you and the family would know about—a song on the radio, an improbable butterfly, a phrase like one he would use: *Well, will you look at that! That's him, all right*, you tell each other—and, as sad as you are, you both laugh. It is as if they were here, part of the conversation still. These things are odd enough that you notice them. I wonder, you say to yourself, I wonder if it is possible that the wall between the worlds is breached sometimes. Might it be that they really can speak to us in their new way, if not in the old one?

They are in Christ, so they do what Christ does: they speak to us in the way we can hear them. That's what the Incarnation is: God coming to us in a way we can understand. Nothing has been added to the Trinity with the birth of Christ: all that has happened is that we have encountered God in a human being who is like us, who holds out hope of our becoming like him. *God became man that man might become God*, Athanasius wrote scandalously, and this is not a thing that happened once and is now over. It is a constant invitation to expand our vision of what it is to be in Christ—an invitation we typically refuse, preferring instead to superimpose our parochial experience of time as linear upon the Incarnation, and upon the Resurrection as well, as if we were talking about something that occurred in the past or will occur in the future. But, though the birth of Jesus of Nazareth did take place at a certain moment in history, the incarnation of Christ encompasses more than the birth of Jesus. His life is not over; it is ongoing. And though the resurrection of Jesus did happen at a time and a place we know, it is not sequestered in the past, either. It, too, is ongoing.

Of course we long for the familiar. Of course we want the dead in their larger existence to remain as they were in this one. We want our connection in the larger life to be just like the one we have in the smaller one. It seems to us that our personality is what makes us ourselves. We treasure our uniqueness, and are apt to overstate its importance. But ancient witnesses encourage us to a wider vision of ourselves: Paul, writing about the Resurrection, compares its mystery to that of a seed:

> As for what you sow, you do not sow the body that is to be, but a bare seed, perhaps of wheat or some other grain.[1]

Jesus does the same, in the gospel of John:

> Very truly, I tell you, unless a grain of wheat falls into the earth and dies, it remains just a single grain; but if it dies, it bears much fruit. Those who love their life lose it, and those who hate their life in this world will keep it for eternal life.[2]

The energetic love of which the universe is made takes many forms. The power of mind is one of them, with its conscious and unconscious faculties of memory, the creation of metaphor, the language of symbol. What we cannot encompass because our words are too small can flow with ease into vessels we *can* talk about. The indescribable life that is larger than this one cannot be spoken in any language we know, but we have always used things we *do* know to bring it forth in metaphor. Christians have often gotten carried away in this endeavor, of course, with our hierarchies of angels, our ornate hells, our heavens like imperial courts or long church services, our imposition of the limited categories of human knowledge upon the unknowable language

1 1 Cor. 15:37.
2 John 12:24–25.

of God: God with a draftsman's compass architecting the universe, God thinking in the language of mathematics, God as a gardener, God as an ancient Near-Eastern king. And, outside the Judeo-Christian orbit, the same human desire to retain familiar categories: the intricacies of reincarnation in Hinduism are another example of an attempt to domesticate the *alsolife* by cutting it down to size and reorganizing it, recycling us, and sorting us according to our correct actions or our misdeeds, with strict attention to the social details of gender and caste. In reincarnation the uniqueness of the self is preserved, even if the individual self has no conscious knowledge of its previous lives. This is so, too, in the ordered but deeply interconnected ancestor worship of Confucian philosophy.

So we take all manner of partial truths for complete ones. It is only human to want to keep what we have, to maintain a permanent place in this world. It is our way of trying to *stay.*

One of our partial truths is our own earthly existence. Ancient Christian thinkers were apt to disparage life in this world. Certainly, we see this in John's hyperbolic statement above about "hating" life in this world. But it isn't the case that earthly life is inferior or unworthy. It's just not the whole story. If we think it is, our deaths are tragic—everything ends. If, though, we invest some thought and contemplation in the observable fact of the conservation of energy—that things don't end, they just change states—we begin to feel more hopeful. The fact of my beloved's existence in a certain time and place expresses itself in many times and places, penetrating my sorrow with familiar images and hints. These are authoritative only to me, but that's all right—you don't need to think that "It Had to Be You" coming on the radio while I'm driving is a message from my mom. I am the only one who needs that. All we need to agree on is that the divine love, that energy of which all things are made and which was contained in her, is free-flowing now. And that my mind assembles it into a form in which I can experience it.

How will you know her? By taking the time while you are here to think about these things. By having the humility to remember that all religious language is metaphor, and that there is more to truth than mere facticity. By allowing your memory of her to expand beyond its pictorial bounds, acknowledging the freedom she now has, unencumbered by time or space. By having the courage to let her come to you in her way, rather than insisting that the language you both spoke then is the only language you will hear from her now. By understanding that this is what it means to be *in Christ*.

If we live in this hopeful way and it turns out that we were mistaken—that there is no divine energy, that the universe is patternless, that the intricate attractions of subatomic particles and enormous stars hold no useful mysteries for us—we are still better off. I lose nothing if I choose to abide in hope. I live out my days to their conclusion. My atheist neighbor does the same. Both of us die, and it turns out there is nothing more. But I had the chance to watch and listen in hope. He did not, having decided in advance that there was nothing to watch or listen for. Neither of us knew for sure—the evidence did not compel assent one way or the other. My hope was not based on evidence. It was a choice, not a conclusion.

I have read that my little Davey O'Day is with me now, in the flesh. Fetal cells can remain in the mother's body for decades, perhaps throughout her life. Like stem cells, they are pluripotential, able to reconfigure themselves to become cells of whatever tissue they join: neurons if they find themselves in the brain, hepatic cells if their new home is in the liver. Some research indicates that these cells may perform an immune function, hastening to a diseased organ and transforming themselves into the new cells it needs.

My little boy flies to my aid. He has attended all my surgeries and helped me heal afterwards. He helped heal the incision for each pacemaker insertion. He slipped into the space between my stent and the arterial wall surrounding it. He inspects my calcifying aortic valve. He does for me all that I could not do for him. He is not a physician, but he is my little boy, still, right here on earth, even though he didn't live long enough ever to hear the word "love." He has met the cells of his two sisters by now, I imagine, and cells of the three of them are alive and busy. There is no significance for those cells in the fact that the girls are living and he is dead.

We think that the kingdom of heaven is far removed from us. We think it unreachable. But the kingdom of heaven is within you, Jesus says. Both are true. Within the painful boundaries with which the passing of time surrounds us—the impenetrable walls between life and death, between love and loss, between youth and age—the timelessness of the kingdom of heaven stands. They exist together.

As I age, it seems that every place I go and everything I do takes me into my past. Here is the parkway exit I took when I was a seminarian at St. Mary's-by-the-Sea. Here on Facebook is my elementary school friend. Here is the recording of the Stravinsky symphony I played over and over again in college. Here is my granddaughter, glancing at me with her mother's eyes. There is Denny and there is Justus, who both have died. The images, the sounds, even the smells settle in softly upon each other like snowflakes, and each one returns something to me that was so lost I had forgotten all about it.

They do not seem unreachable; on the contrary, they are richly present. Whether they are current or in the past is of surprisingly little significance to me. I think I am getting to be a little like Davey O'Day.

I wonder if this means I am soon to die myself? Well, of

course I am—I have lived much more of my life than I have yet to live. This prospect, too, is of modest significance to me now: it is nowhere near as unthinkable, for instance, as the prospect of my mother's death was before it occurred decades ago. Soon to die? Well, who knows? None of us.

But ready to die? Sure. The world owes me no more life than it has already given me. The gift of life has been astounding in its generosity. A fraction of it would have been more than enough. As it is, my cup runneth over.

CHAPTER 7

UNLIKELY MYSTICS

> All mystics . . . speak the same language and come from the same country. As against that fact, the place which they happen to occupy in the kingdom of this world matters little.
>
> —Louis Claude de Saint-Martin, ca. 1790

From where we sit, we don't discern many avenues of approach to the *alsolife*. Imagining the past, the present, and the future all smashed together to create a simultaneous NOW does not come naturally to us. We try to fathom it, but slip back again and again onto the path we know best, the linear one-thing-after-another model of the world as we experience it on a superficial level. And why wouldn't we? This view works well for us almost all the time. It is so efficient at organizing our experience that we usually discount the hints we get of a more complex reality—dreams, déjà vu, the timelessness we enter in centering prayer, the oneness we sometimes feel with another person.

But the linearity we know and love doesn't work all the time. It doesn't explain everything. There are things we cannot know in the ways in which we usually come to know things, and it is human nature to want to know.

There is a large and venerable body of testimony to a more dimensional approach in the record of mystical experience, going back centuries. Long before the term *space-time* had been coined, people journeyed across the borders of time and location in prayer, and they wrote about it. These were monastics, for the most part, people who spent at least five hours a day in prayer, often much more. Writing from within the rigors of the enclosed life, confined in so many ways, they nonetheless report a freedom we do not enjoy.

The fact that their lives were so different from ours makes most people think that such spiritual freedom is not available to those of us who don't live medieval lives in medieval convents. We think the vision of a life larger than the one we know is given only to a few. This is not so. Everyone who has ever fallen asleep and dreamed has ventured toward it. Anyone can learn to recognize it.

It is time to talk about prayer.

Insofar as I was taught about prayer as a child, I was given to understand it primarily as asking for things. I was to ask God to bless my parents and my brothers and my grandmothers, both of whom lived with us. As my grandmothers sickened and then died, I added cures for cancer and heart disease to my requests. For a brief period, I asked that my father not be transferred to Alabama, and kept it up until the danger was over. I don't recall praying for good grades in school—I suppose I felt praying for something that was within my own power to achieve wasn't quite the thing. Prayer needed to be about things clearly beyond my control.

When did I begin to suspect that there might be more to prayer than making requests? I learned in confirmation class that there were five types of prayer: adoration, penitence, petition, thanksgiving, and intercession. The differences among them were differences relating to my posture and goals. Was I guilty? In need of something? If I was not consciously grateful, it was pointed out to me that there was always something to be thankful for and that I should cultivate gratitude by thanking God for something every time I prayed. I saw that this was indeed the case, set out to do it, and have done it ever since. If I was not feeling overwhelmed by God's glory at a particular time, I was reminded that God's glory was nonetheless steadily present in the universe and that it would be a good idea to mention it consistently in prayer. My prayerful allusions to God's glory were consistent but they were also rather dutiful, except on those occasions when I really *was* overwhelmed by God's glory, which was usually in connection with something in the natural world. In all these cases, it was clear that I was in some way addressing God. There was a space between us, but I was within hailing distance.

I was not given information about how and when God might contact *me*. We did have films in Sunday school in which God spoke to people in the Bible—they were tableaux, not motion pictures, so we were able to stare for minutes at a time at actors playing Jeremiah or Peter or Joseph, transfixed at the voice of God while the narrator read the relevant Scripture to us. Often the film would zoom in for a close-up of the same motionless encounter, to emphasize a certain phrase we were hearing. Oh, my—what I would give to see those films now, as an adult! But it was slow going at best. I expected that the voice of God, should I ever be privileged to hear it, would be slow and sonorous like that, and I expected that there would be plenty of time to react. Indeed, very little reaction seemed called for: It looked like all you had to do was stand very still and look thunderstruck.

I did want more. I continued to want more into my young adult years, as foolishly preoccupied as I was with the blind alleys to which I devoted so much time and energy and from which I harvested so much trouble. I could no longer pray my old shopping list from childhood—I recognized that it was completely self-centered. Often I heard within me a voice informing me snidely that in actuality I *had* no faith, that I was faking the whole thing. This was alarming. What if it were true?

It was in this period, when I was quite wrong-headed and not at all prepared, that God contacted me unmistakably. How do I know that? I cannot tell you, not in any way that would compel your belief. But I can tell you what happened. I was in bed, thinking about prayer. That is, I *think* I was thinking about prayer—this was nearly fifty years ago now, so I might have been thinking about something else. But I was quiet, and I was alone. Then, for what seemed like a moment—a split second—I felt the power of the universe pass through a small portion of my right arm. The power of everything that is. I can still touch the place where it passed through me. I will show you, if we ever meet. But you won't be able to see anything.

Things that did not happen:

> I did not do everything right after that.
>
> I did not understand the event itself.

Things that did happen:

> I never forgot it.
>
> I never doubted that it was real.

I *told* you it would not compel your belief. But it compelled mine.

Perhaps the efforts of the mystics to explain their experience to us fails to compel assent, but it encourages each of us to hope for the moment that will accomplish in us what their moment did in them. If so, as halting as they are—almost meaningless, as mine was—they are stories worth telling.

Here is Julian of Norwich in the fourteenth century, never venturing from her cell built onto the side of the church, with a window looking into it through which she could receive communion. Her radical experience of complete oneness with God seems to her to fit without a wrinkle into what she has been taught about the Trinity, but her imagination within this ancient framework is extraordinarily free.

> And I saw no difference between God and our substance, but, as it were, all God; and still my understanding accepted that our substance is in God, that is to say that God is God, and our substance is a creature in God. For the almighty truth of the Trinity is our Father, for he made us and he keeps us in him. And the deep wisdom of the Trinity is our Mother, in whom we are enclosed. And the high goodness of the Trinity is our Lord, and in him we are enclosed and he in us. We are enclosed in the Father, and we are enclosed in the Son, and we are enclosed in the Holy Spirit. And the Father is enclosed in us, the Son is enclosed in us, and the Holy Spirit is enclosed in us, almighty, all wisdom and goodness, one God, one Lord.[1]

Here is the brisk and orderly mind of Teresa of Avila, applying itself to a description of her mystical experiences,

1 Julian of Norwich, *Revelations of the Divine Love*, Chapter 54.

which for a period in her life seem to have been rather frequent. Note that she specifically rejects the use of the term *vision*. She wants it understood that her experiences were concrete and physically real.

> I used unexpectedly to experience a consciousness of the presence of God, of such a kind that I could not possibly doubt that He was within me or that I was wholly engulfed in Him. This was in no sense a vision: I believe it is called mystical theology. The soul is suspended in such a way that it seems to be completely outside itself. The will loves; the memory, I think, is almost lost; while the understanding, I believe, though it is not lost, does not reason—I mean that it does not work, but is amazed at the extent of all it can understand; for God wills it to realize that it understands nothing of what His Majesty represents to it.[2]

During the time when these experiences we're not supposed to call visions were occurring, Teresa was also busy doing other things—founding seventeen convents, corresponding with popes and kings, writing books. The monastics whose mystical visions we read about in the accounts they have left us all arise from within a corporate framework of very orthodox behavior and thought. They lived in community. A bell rang and they hurried to the chapel, day after day and year after year, to repeat words that they had long since learned by heart, just from repeating them so often. It was not the freshness of a new liturgy that carried them into their glimpse of the *alsolife*; their days were surrounded and shaped by the old one. Their experience did not arise from revolutionary thinking, but seemed to them to confirm what they had inherited from their tradition.

2 *Life of St. Teresa of Jesus, of The Order of Our Lady of Carmel*, written by St. Teresa of Avila, chap. 10.

We know who the famous mystics are: Julian of Norwich, Richard Rolle, Hildegard of Bingen, Meister Eckhart, Teresa, John of the Cross, the author of *The Cloud of Unknowing*, others. But we ordinarily *don't* include Paul of Tarsus on the list of Christian mystics. He is famous, but not for that. Paul was an ill-tempered persecutor of Christians before he became one. After that, he was an ill-tempered Christian. He founded churches in a number of cities, and wrote letters to them afterward. Most of his letters contained at least one scolding; a few of them contained little else. It is easy to forget that this cranky person was also a mystic. But here he recounts an experience of a person quite unlike the Paul we thought we knew—he speaks in the third person here, but it is clear from the context that he is talking about himself. Poor Paul—hypersensitive to other Christians' understandable criticism about his past, he is unable to resist using even his experience of heaven to score points in his steady battle to be seen by them as an apostle as legitimate as those who had walked with Jesus of Nazareth.

> I know a person in Christ who fourteen years ago was caught up to the third heaven—whether in the body or out of the body I do not know; God knows. And I know that such a person—whether in the body or out of the body I do not know; God knows—was caught up into Paradise and heard things that are not to be told, that no mortal is permitted to repeat. I will boast about a man like that, but I will not boast about myself, except about my weaknesses. Even if I should choose to boast, I would not be a fool, because I would be speaking the truth. But I refrain, so no one will think more of me than is warranted by what I do or say, or because of these surpassingly great revelations.[3]

3 2 Cor. 12:2–7.

This ecstatic vision is not what we remember first about Paul. That would be his moral theology, probably, or his vision of the Resurrection. Certainly his missionary energy. But these indescribable moments are part of him, too, important enough to write about, in an age when writing was never an idle pastime. Paul remembers exactly when this unforgettable event occurred—it was fourteen years before he wrote this letter. He can't find words to express much else. Was he in the body or out? He doesn't know. He heard things but cannot repeat them for us. Thus, the certifying power of such an experience for anybody besides Paul himself is limited: whatever his mystical journey meant, it cannot be fully shared. We know of other experiences in which the laws upon which temporal reality is based were suspended: his own conversion, in which he hears the voice of Jesus and is struck blind, his vision of a Macedonian man asking for his help for the church there, his description of his own speaking in tongues, his prayer in "sighs too deep for words."[4]

We are not the people of Paul's generation. We trust only that which we can explain, and are apt to imagine that we have understood something completely when we have found a physical or psychological basis for it, as if the entirety of a phenomenon were comprehended because we know its origin. We are apt to take the beginning of our understanding for the whole of it. *That was just a dream*, we say when we awaken from one, *and a dream is not real*. Our psychotherapists help us see what longing or fear might have given rise to the dream. All helpful and all true.

But not the whole truth of the dream. The longing or the fear or the love or the anger—these are facts, too. Our past is a fact, and our future is a fact as well—whether a dream pictures these with journalistic accuracy or with metaphor, the

4 Acts 9:1–19, Acts 16:9, 1 Cor. 14:14–19, Rom. 8:26.

past has indeed happened and the future will indeed unfold, and our dream places us within their orbit. Our engagement with them is a chemical fact about us, we now know, an *electrical* fact, even—different parts of our brains light up like Christmas trees when we think, or when we experience an emotion. And, although they are difficult to put into words, there is enough tradition of taking our mystical moments seriously, stretching through enough time, that such moments are recognizable within the tradition of mystical experience. Many people, each in his or her own way, groping for adequate words and settling for inadequate ones, have written about the mystical union with Christ using the tools of their own experiences—their dreams, their meditation, their encounters with the natural world, their prayer, and their participation in the sacraments.

That this record of human experience could simply be a mistake with an extraordinarily long run is certainly a possibility, but it is not the only possibility. There could actually be an encounter with existence itself, an encounter human beings can have, one which gives us glimpses of the *alsolife*, the limitless reality within which our own limited reality rests.

We don't remember Augustine as a mystic, either. We know him as the inventor of Original Sin, as the great theologian of the Trinity, as the complex forerunner of psychoanalytic insights that would not bear fruit for another fifteen hundred years. His *Confessions,* still read by college students today, was the first genuine autobiography—a millennium would pass before there was a second. His fourth-century *City of God* was completely at home amid the bleak Cold War realism of the mid-twentieth century. If anyone was ever a thinker for the ages, it was he.

We don't think of him as a contemplative. But here he is, remembering a conversation with his mother on their retreat in the port city of Ostia, shortly before her death. They are sitting in a window of their house:

> And when our conversation had brought us to the point where the very highest of physical sense and the most intense illumination of physical light seemed, in comparison with the sweetness of that life to come, not worthy of comparison, nor even of mention, we lifted ourselves with a more ardent love toward the Selfsame, and we gradually passed through all the levels of bodily objects, and even through the heaven itself . . . . Indeed, we soared higher yet by an inner musing, speaking and marveling at thy works. And we came at last to our own minds and went beyond them . . . .
>
> And while we were thus speaking and straining after her [Wisdom] we just barely touched her with the whole effort of our hearts. Then with a sigh, leaving the first fruits of the Spirit bound to that ecstasy, we returned to the sounds of our own tongue, where the spoken word had both beginning and end.[5]

They spoke of physical things, of light, of heaven, higher and higher, until words failed them and finally became unnecessary. Augustine's mystical experience ascended through physical reality into the realm of mind and then of spirit and then of existence itself. This is the language of the Platonic ascent, from physical experience to spiritual experience to oneness with God, as Paul's was in the language of his Jewish cosmology, as Julian's was in the language of the Trinity—all of us use the words we have available from the place and time in which we live. Those who enter experiences such as these remark afterwards upon the inadequacy of language in their attempts to describe them. But they all keep talking. That moment is impossible to describe, but the mystics seem compelled to try.

5 *Confessions* 9.10.

The Paul we know was a revolutionary, sweeping aside many things he and others held sacred, often paying a high price for doing so. Orthodoxy of theology and practice has been so consistent a fact in the lives of so many of the mystics that most of us imagine it to be a requirement, as if one could be either a mystic or a revolutionary, but not both. I can recall conversations with activist clergy who disparaged the very word "spirituality," believing that it meant turning one's back on the pain of the world. And I can recall conversations with people of prayer who believed strongly that a Christian should never be involved in politics. But I have known many people, both monastic and lay, who have married these two perspectives in their own lives. Liberation theology often is set against mystical theology in the minds of those who have superficial acquaintance with one or both, but it need not be so.

Those who long for the transformation of this world have spiritual lives, too. Like Paul or Augustine or Julian or you or me, they speak of their encounter with God in the language of both their milieu and their experience, which places a liberation theologian squarely within the context of oneness with humanity, without which they do not see oneness with God as possible—or even desirable. In this, they remind me of nobody more than the bitter Ivan in *The Brothers Karamazov*, though they can be far more hopeful than Ivan was, born too soon in an era which offered no resonance to his anguished cry for justice.

Here is liberation theologian Dorothee Soelle, socialist, peace activist, and revered theologian of the Protestant left wing:

> For me, mysticism and transformation are indissolubly interconnected. Without economic and ecological justice . . . and without God's preferential love

> for the poor and for this planet, the love for God and the longing for oneness seem to me to be an atomistic illusion. The spark of the soul acquired in private experience may indeed serve the search for gnosis in the widest sense of the word, but it can do no more. Genuine mystical journey has a much larger goal than to teach us positive thinking and put to sleep our capacity to be critical and to suffer.[6]

What we know now about the energy of God's love buttresses such a conviction. Not only is the stuff of the earth made of God's love; our relationships are made of it as well. The energy of human to human is the energy of God, as is the energy between animals, plants, the earth itself. The things we may have thought profane are really holy, and it falls to us to recognize this as true and to show it forth. Here is Dorothy Day, pacifist, activist on behalf of the poor, co-founder of the *Catholic Worker*:

> It is because we forget the Humanity of Christ (present with us today in the Blessed Sacrament just as truly as when He walked with His apostles through the cornfields that Sunday long ago, breakfasting on the ears of corn)—that we have ignored the material claims of our fellow man during this capitalistic, industrialist era . . . . This ignoring of the material body of our humanity which Christ ennobled when He took flesh, gives rise to the aversion for religion evidenced by many workers. As a result of this worshipping of the Divinity alone of Christ and ignoring His Sacred Humanity, religious people looked to Heaven for justice and Karl Marx could say—"Religion is the opium of the people."[7]

6 Dorothee Soelle, *The Silent Cry: Mysticism and Resistance*, 88–93.

7 Dorothy Day, *The Catholic Worker*, June 1935, 4.

As Julian felt a visceral oneness with God, which she expressed in Trinitarian terms, Day finds oneness with Christ through solidarity with humanity expressed in sacramental language.

> When we pray with Christ . . . we realize Christ as our Brother. We think of all men as our brothers then, as members of the Mystical Body of Christ. "We are all members, one of another," and, remembering this, we can never be indifferent to the social miseries and evils of the day. The dogma of the Mystical Body has tremendous social implications.
>
> We are our brothers' keeper, and all men are our brothers whether they are Catholic or not. But of course the tie that binds Catholics is closer, the tie of grace. We partake of the same food, Christ. We put off the old man and put on Christ. The same blood flows through our veins, Christ's. We are the same flesh, Christ's. But all men are members or potential members, as St. Augustine says, and there is no time with God, so who are we to know the degree of separation between us and the Communist, the unbaptized, the God-hater, who may tomorrow, like St. Paul, love Christ.

Thomas Merton wrote *Conjectures of a Guilty Bystander* in 1966, with the Vietnam War in full fury. His time in the Trappist Gethsemani Abbey seemed to him at first to be a flight from the world into an enclosed life of silence and prayer, but his writings from the beginning of his vocation kept him much more in contact with life outside the monastery walls than he ever thought he would be.

His friendship with Dorothy Day was through letters; they never met in the flesh. Though his vocation was a different one from hers, he admired her greatly, and once told her that the *Catholic Worker*'s radical witness among the poor was a significant part of what drew him to the Catholic Church. Day's absolutist activism met Merton's more untried pacifism, offering it a steady challenge and widening his spiritual focus to include the world he never really left behind, prompting him to explore it further. The mystical union with the world he felt in this famous passage was not inner peace alone; it carried a promise for the peace of the world.

> In Louisville, at the corner of Fourth and Walnut, in the center of the shopping district, I was suddenly overwhelmed with the realization that I loved all these people, that they were mine and I theirs, that we could not be alien to one another even though we were total strangers. It was like waking from a dream of separateness, of spurious self-isolation in a special world . . . . Then it was as if I suddenly saw the secret beauty of their hearts, the depths of their hearts where neither sin nor desire nor self-knowledge can reach, the core of their reality, the person that each one is in God's eyes. If only they could all see themselves as they really are. If only we could see each other that way all the time. There would be no more war, no more hatred, no more cruelty, no more greed.[8]

I loved Merton and Dorothy Day—I didn't know they knew each other, and it pleases me now to learn that they did, and that the way they knew each other was the way I know them both, through their writing. I loved Augustine—I wrote my undergraduate thesis on him. I loved Paul—his crankiness is what I love most about him, I think: If he could be that touchy and get in the Bible, there must be hope for me. I loved Dorothee

8 Thomas Merton, *Conjectures of a Guilty Bystander.*

Soelle—her book *Suffering* saved my life during my own Ivan Karamazov period. I loved all these people when I was young. I love them still today. The centuries between us mattered not at all to me then, and they don't matter now. All of them are dead now. I myself am on my way out. Life is brief—a candle, a plucked flower that fades before our eyes.

We need to touch the *alsolife*, even if we can touch it only briefly. We need to let our imaginations carry us to the edge of it and then let go of us. If we live a life of which prayer and wonder is a part, we will already know what it is to feel time collapse into insignificance. There will come a time when we will need this knowledge.

CHAPTER 8

THE LOVE OF GOD IS ENERGY

Time is elastic. The linearity of time is only how we mark it: it is not how we experience it. It is a model of reality; it is not reality itself. We may describe time in a narrative line, but we experience it only in moments. We may glue our moments together with memory, but we live them one by one.

Matter is the same way. Our perception of it is really a model, a shorthand way of arranging the energy of creation. Here is your desk. It is made of wood, solid as a rock. You rap on it with your knuckles and get a reassuringly solid knock. This desk is inert. It is inorganic. It is motionless. Now you tap on your own chest. You feel your flesh yield a bit, but you also feel the hard bones of your ribs. You are solid, too.

But you are not as solid as your desk. Of course not, you say. I am alive. I am organic. Within me, even when I sit perfectly still, millions of cells divide and reproduce. Blood courses through my veins, electric impulses traverse my nerves. I am in constant motion. I will never be still. Even in death, motion within me will continue, life in different forms contained within the framework of my body. Oh, yes—there are animals in there right now. My body is a busy community of living things.

You turn to your desk again and give it another rap with your knuckles. It doesn't move. But you know that it, too, is teeming with motion: molecular motion and atomic energy within each molecule. The constituent particles of each atom hurtle through what, to them, are great expanses of open space—most of your desk, like most of everything else, is space. The space between. The colossal energy of the atom keeps them from flying apart.

And the difference between the organic and the inorganic is vast to us, but not to the God in whom it is all created. We are all made of the same substance, after all—the tremendous energy breaking and breaking into the universe, creating it as it goes. Energy and matter are really different forms of the same thing—notwithstanding the many forms it takes, the energetic word of God is really all there is. *Let there be light*—and there is light. From that word flows everything that is.

The energy of the creation is what the love of God is.

Wait. What?

The energy of the creation is what the love of God is.

The love of God isn't God feeling a certain way about us. It isn't God liking or disliking us. It isn't that kind of love. It is

God creating us, steadily speaking creation into being. We are made of the love of God. We are not separate from God. We are part of God, though mostly we don't know it.

I love the Beatles.

I love crème brûlée.

I love Giotto's paintings.

I love the movie *Casablanca.*

I love my family.

I love you.

These are human loves. In all of them, I am the subject and love is the verb. In all of them, the things I love are direct objects, things upon which my love acts. These loves are appreciative, admiring the excellence of their objects. They are erotic—and we can remind ourselves here that, in philosophy, the word *erotic* is not confined to sexual love, though it includes it. All sexual love is erotic, but not all erotic love is sexual. Erotic love is love that desires to possess its object. In both of these loves, appreciative and erotic, the object of my love is separate from me.

God's love is neither appreciative nor erotic.

Appreciative love is conditional, based upon the good qualities of the beloved. I taste a spoonful of crème brûlée. If it has spoiled from sitting out too long, it won't taste good, and then I won't love it any more. Appreciative love is not a permanent state; it bases itself upon the conformity of the beloved to a standard of excellence external to itself. It ends when that conformity ends.

Erotic love is also not a permanent state. Its existence depends upon dissatisfaction. It is essential that I never possess my beloved fully; I need to remain hungry and thirsty for him. Should my hunger end, my love will not be not far behind. Hymns to erotic love, whether secular or sacred, often posit a future time when love will be satisfied but will continue, its strength and character unchanged and unabated. But erotic love can't do that: *eros* is powered by deprivation.

Many of the psalms sing of God's love in erotic or appreciative terms, as if they were like the human loves I have mentioned—my love for crème brûlée, for *Casablanca*, for my lover.

> As the deer longs for the waterbrooks,
> so longs my soul for you, O God.
>
> Psalm 42:1
>
> I love you Lord, my strength.
>
> Psalm 18:1
>
> O God, you are my God; earnestly I seek you;
> my soul thirsts for you; my flesh faints for you,
> as in a dry and weary land where there is no water.
>
> Psalm 63:1

So does the Song of Songs, when read as an allegory of the soul's longing for God. The language is extravagant, as love poetry often is. But the mutuality of love in the Song is striking: each seeks the other passionately, rejoices fully in the other.

She speaks

> I am a rose of Sharon, a lily of the valleys.

He speaks

> As a lily among brambles, so is my love among maidens.

She speaks

> As an apple tree among the trees of the wood, so is my beloved among young men. With great delight I sat in his shadow, and his fruit was sweet to my taste. He brought

> me to the banqueting house, and his intention toward me was love. Sustain me with raisins, refresh me with apples; for I am faint with love. O that his left hand were under my head, and that his right hand embraced me![1]

Or this:

He speaks

> I compare you, my love, to a mare among Pharaoh's chariots. Your cheeks are comely with ornaments, your neck with strings of jewels. We will make you ornaments of gold, studded with silver.

She speaks

> While the king was on his couch, my nard gave forth its fragrance. My beloved is to me a bag of myrrh that lies between my breasts.

He speaks

> My beloved is to me a cluster of henna blossoms in the vineyards of En-gedi. Ah, you are beautiful, my love; ah, you are beautiful; your eyes are doves.

Certainly the fact that it was a wedding song before it was anything else explains the mutual excitement we find in the Song. But knowing how something began doesn't mean we understand the whole of it. The Song's inclusion in the canon of Scripture for millennia tells us that people have understood it to be more than a wedding song for a long, long time. The Song is in the Bible because we can read it as if it were about God's love for us and our love for God. It may not have been about the love of God when it was written, but it is now.

The mutuality of the Song stands in contrast to Bernini's one-sided *Ecstasy of St. Teresa* in the church of Santa Maria della Vittoria in Rome, the orgasmic baroque masterpiece

1 Song of Sol. 2:1–6.

before which Italian schoolboys have stood and snickered for nearly four centuries. Well, of course it does—they were created some two thousand years apart in two very different cultures and in completely different media. But their subject is the same: the love of God.

Bernini, *Ecstasy of St. Teresa*, 1647–52,
Church of Santa Maria della Vittoria, Rome

The statue depicts the saint ravished by God's love, her head fallen backward, her eyes closed, her lips apart. God's love, in the person of the angel, is the subject, not Teresa. She is the object of God's love, and God's love is like human love: possessive. She is overwhelmed by it; she cannot move. The instrument by which the mystical union is accomplished is an arrow. The angel wielding it is a Christian version of Cupid, son of Eros, armed with the tools of an ancient hunter or soldier—another classical figure borrowed for the occasion, like the blindfolded figure of Justice we discussed earlier. The angel's face is a conundrum: his smile is a knowing and somehow distant one. He is aware of his victim's readiness to receive his dart, almost amused by it. Given the famously profound emotion on Teresa's face, the angel's distant regard—friendly though it is—gives one pause. Teresa is transported; the angel is not.

Two different works of art from two different places and times. There are many others whose names I could have dropped instead. Most theologians of the church's first four centuries wrote commentaries on the Song of Songs. So did most medieval theologians: the Venerable Bede, Bernard of Clairvaux, Hildegaard of Bingen, Anselm, to name a mere handful. Thomas Aquinas is said to have spoken a commentary on it from his deathbed, and it was the Song he asked to be read to him in his last hour.

But is it God's love for us or our love for God? Who is active?

Honk if you love Jesus.

If you love Jesus, paste this into your status bar and share.

O, how I love Jesus, O, how I love Jesus, O, how I love Jesus, because he first loved me. We sang this song when I was a child. Miss Bessie Forwood played the wheezy little organ in our new parish hall every Sunday for us, while the adults were listening to the sermon up in the church.

Jesus loves me, this I know, for the Bible tells me so. We sang that one, too. Karl Barth once said that it summed up his theology perfectly.

A woman comes to see me. *I just don't feel love for Jesus. I don't know how. I can't see or hear or touch him, but I'm supposed to love him? I feel guilty every time they talk about loving Jesus in church, and they do it all the time—so they must be able to feel it. God the Father, I get—creator. Mother is fine by me, too—I've got three kids, and I know something about creation. I look around me at the beautiful world and I get God the creator. God the Holy Spirit, I also get—that's the breath of life. Jesus's moral teaching and healing, dying and rising: I do respect it all. But how do I love him?*

Mary Magdalene reaches out to touch the risen Jesus. He rebuffs her. *Do not touch me,* he says, *for I have not yet ascended to the Father* (John 20:17). This moment was so arresting that the many paintings of it throughout the centuries that have passed since the moment itself are all called *Noli me tangere*—Touch me not. It is probably the post-resurrection appearance most frequently portrayed in Western art. An unknown Spanish carver created this beauty in 1090.

Unknown artist, *Noli me tangere*, wooden plaque, Spanish, ca. 1060

And here is Giotto's, early in the fourteenth century, in the Scrovegni Chapel in Padua.

Giotto, *Noli me tangere*, Scrovegni Chapel, Padua, ca. 1305

Caraciollo in 1620 also gives Christ a gardener's hat and a scythe—both had become a commonplace by then. Mary Magdalene reaches for him in a way that suggests a sexual advance: although Jesus's and Mary's hands are always high and low in these paintings, hers are not so precisely aimed or so near his body in other painters' versions. In this painting her hand reaches toward his genitals, while his hand directs her higher. Caraciollo, like everyone else in his day and too many in our own, must have accepted the misplaced identification of Mary Magdalene with a repentant prostitute as fact.

Caraciollo, *Noli me tangere*, Museo Civico, Prato, ca. 1620.

But why? Why should she not touch him? Certainly they have loved each other, in a relationship more mutual than some people in the early church were willing to believe—and regardless of what movies we may have seen, we need not obsess here about whether or not it was a romantic one to affirm its importance. When we speak of the love of God, do we mean our love for God or God's love for us? And if it's our love for God, is it like the other loves we know about? Do we love God like we love our children? Our lovers? Mary Magdalene tries to relate to the risen Christ in the old way, but that can no longer be. *Do not touch me.*

So what is it? How do we love God? How does God love us?

We try to apply our familiar categories of love to our relationship with God, but fall short. None of them bring us near enough: the most mutual of human loves cannot bridge the gap between two people. We may be able to finish each other's sentences, I may know every detail of his life before we met, but here on the earth, we will always be separate. There will always be space between us.

God's love—both God's love for us and ours for God, as we will see—is not like that. There is no space between us in the kingdom of heaven. All of the paintings of it you have seen—the thrones, the streets paved with gold, the glassy sea, the golden-crowned saints, the winged angels: they are paintings of a metaphor, not descriptions of reality. Heaven is not a place in which we become flawless versions of our earthly selves. What is overcome in heaven is our separateness. The love of God draws us together with God and, because it draws us all, it joins us to one another.

Here is Thomas Aquinas:

> For it is evident that by the very nature of the action what is loved is in the one who loves. Therefore whoever loves God possesses God in himself; for scripture says, Whoever remains in love remains in God and God in him. It is the nature of love to transform the lover into the object loved. And so if we love God, we ourselves become divinized; for again, Whoever is joined to God becomes one spirit with him. [2]

It is the nature of love to transform the lover into the object loved.

This is what incarnation is: it is love. The lover becomes the beloved. *The Word became flesh and dwelt among us.* And resurrection is its corollary—the beloved becomes the lover. *God*

2 "*Opuscula*, In duo praecenta . . . ," ed. J. P. Torrel, *Revue des Sc. Phil. Et Théol.* 69 (1985): 26–29.

became human that humankind might become God. In the end, whether the love of God is our love for God or God's love for us becomes an unnecessary question. The distinction between the two disappears. There is no lover and there is no beloved. There is only love.

You remember a dime-store toy back when we were children. It was a cardboard rectangle with human face on it and a clear concave plastic shield over the face. Inside the shield were iron filings, and it came with a magnet. You passed the magnet over the shield and the iron filings would follow it. You could give the face a beard or a mustache, different haircuts. You could make it a girl or a boy.

I loved playing with it. Making the different faces and hairstyles was fun, of course, but before long I lost interest in the face. It was the iron filings themselves that entranced me: the magnet could move them without touching them. They followed it wherever it went, piling one on top of another in their eagerness. Let them escape from beneath their plastic shield—as I had been known to do—and you could make a tower of them on the tabletop: up and up they would climb, drawn by their attraction to the magnet. They even clung to *each other* when the magnet passed over them, as if they had become magnets themselves—as, in fact, they had.

It is the nature of love to transform the lover into the object loved.

The love of God is energy. It is like the magnet—indeed, the magnet's attractive energy is the same energy as the love of God. The love of God is energy, the singular energy that created and creates the universe. There *is* no other energy. Everything that exists is made of it. The energy, which is God, creates matter out of itself, and with itself gives order to matter. Colossal energy exists within the atom, keeping it from flying apart—this is why nuclear power is so great, why an atomic bomb the size of a suitcase could level a city. No wonder we are sobered by the power of nuclear energy—we know that we are tinkering with the power of the universe itself.

The woman who couldn't love Jesus was trying to apply the limited categories of human love to something else. Is he handsome enough, kind enough, attentive enough, powerful enough? Do I love him because he is the smartest, biggest, strongest? Do I have the same emotions I had when I fell in love with a human being? No wonder she didn't succeed, and it was not her fault: the narrow vision of our culture has schooled her in a narrow vision of love, a love both appreciative and erotic but with no other categories that might take her further and deeper. If we seek the signs of the love, instead of the love itself, we will not find them. I may want the ecstasy I see on Teresa's face, but I won't get it by seeking ecstasy. *Noli me tangere. Because it won't get you where you want to go.*

We don't need to love Jesus like a boyfriend. He doesn't need to be our buddy or our copilot or our lawyer or our agent. Not that any of those modes of loving are wrong—nobody's going to be punished for feeling the love of Jesus or for using familiar images to imagine him. Who doesn't want to have powerful feelings of love? But we must be aware that they are feelings attached to metaphor, not fact. Human ways of loving may model the love of God for us, but they fall short of its fullness. Human desires can draw us, but they are not necessary—life in Christ is more than an emotive state. We can relax and stop trying to conjure up romantic or filial feelings about God if they elude us. The attraction of God is sufficient to draw us, in whatever emotive state we find ourselves.

There is a trinity of the human being, like the trinity of God. We are intellect, we are emotion, and we are will—all three are who we are. Minimize any one of them and we become monstrous. Our capacity for reason enables us to reflect upon the world and, crucially, upon ourselves. Our feelings motivate us toward some things and away from others. Our will makes us able to act in ways other than as our feelings prompt us. We may consider love a matter of emotion, but a human being is more than just a bag of feelings. Disastrous things can happen when we try to confine even love of another human being to that arena; why would loving God be any more possible as an emotional project alone?

This is not to say that we should declare war on our feelings. They are part of us, too, like our reason and our will, and they can make life sweet for us—when they're not making it awful. It is simply to state that our emotions, happy or sad, are not the whole of us. The energy that created and creates the universe (for creation is an ongoing process, not a one-time event) continues to attract us. We are drawn to it, for we are part of it. We can't help it: We came from it and we return to it. It draws us like the magnet draws the iron filings. Pass the toy magnet over the plastic screen again, and watch the iron filings as they twitch, longing to leap. They stretch every nerve in their desire to unite with that which attracts them. We also long to leap toward God, our original energy, whether we know it or not. All our other longings, however mundane, are forms of that energetic longing. We are drawn by that magnet; in being drawn by it, we become magnets ourselves, as the iron filings do. It is our nature to be drawn, as it is God's nature to draw us. And the whole of us is drawn in that pull—our reason, our will and our feelings. One or two of them may lag behind, but the entirety of us is drawn, and we get there in the end. The whole of us is pulled into the energetic love of God and by its power running through us, we draw others to it.

It is the nature of love to transform the lover into the object loved.

One of the things we would have to give up if we were to

live into this nature would be our conviction that this attractive love is conditional upon our response. That will be difficult for many, as you will recall from our discussion of hell a few chapters ago. A football fan raises a hand-lettered sign for the television camera to see: JOHN 3:16, it says, which is shorthand for *God so loved the world that He gave His only begotten Son, to the end that all that believe on Him should not perish, but have eternal life.* Convinced that a scheme of reward and punishment was necessary to enable human beings to stay on the good side of an anthropomorphic deity, the notion of a God bound by the necessity of a correct human response before he could act grew steadily more ironclad, encasing the freedom of God in an unyielding shell of unbreakable rules. The story of salvation long ago became a strictly personal matter, a drama about the sins and virtues of individuals.

A story:

The Puritan pilgrims who settled in the Plymouth Bay Colony came there in order to establish a society congruent with their religious beliefs, free from the molestation of the Church of England. Central to their theology was the conviction that salvation belonged only to the elect, and that there would be clear evidence in a person's life, readily discernible to him, that he was part of that happy band. He would be able to recount a moment when that membership became a certainty. The rest of humanity was bound for another place.

There they were, an ocean away from their homes in England: a pilgrim band who had all experienced the same profound moment of conversion. The cost of their discipleship was high. They endured cold, hunger, and disease in order to live in this way. Half of them died in the first year. But they persevered, supporting each other in the life they had chosen, disciplining one another when that life faltered and teaching their children the tenets of the faith in which they passionately believed. Life was still hard, but it was theirs. But after a fashion, they prospered.

The children who were born in the colony as time went by had never known life in England. They had no experience of what it was to be a dissenting minority—here, they *were* the dominant culture, and there *was* no minority. They grew to adulthood under the unchallenged tutelage of their parents' stern faith, absorbing it with their mothers' milk. Thus, the opportunity to have a life-changing moment of conversion was not as easy to come by. It is hard to convert to a life one is already living.

This presented families with a terrible conundrum. Damnation was a lurid certainty to all human beings not chosen by God to be saved from it. Salvation was impossible without the certainty of election, and a definite movement from one state to another, a clear moment of having been "born again." Evidence of this having occurred was necessary for full membership in the church, and their children could not produce it. The congregation faced dwindling prospects if the number of people who could be fully participating members of it did not increase as the first pilgrim generations died out, and this had large practical consequences for the colony.

They loved their children and they believed in their faith. What hope might they secure that did not endanger one or the other?

Love won over rigor this time, and a way was found: the Halfway Covenant, a plan by which a person who had not yet experienced the second birth could become a full member until such time as he experienced it, which would surely come. There were those who vehemently objected to such a softening of discipline. For the time being, they did not prevail.

From a distance, the Puritans may look absurd, impaled upon their own insistence on a certain kind of individual experience as the only one that counted. But to this day, the language of salvation reflects the individualism rampant in Western culture: it is common to hear that someone has "accepted Jesus Christ as my personal savior." I suppose that if one can have a personal assistant, a personal trainer and even a personal shopper, a personal savior makes some sense. But it is a long walk from that self-absorbed transaction to the great sweep of love that creates a universe and holds it together.

The same energy that creates the world creates us. It is infinite. I have called that energy the love of God, and we have distinguished it from other loves. The divine love is not sentiment in one being directed at another, but energy that both enfolds and animates all things. All energy and all matter are in the love of God.

What does it mean, then, when I say that I will pray for you? Certainly it cannot mean that I am conjuring, uttering the incantation that will induce God to grant my request. Nor can it mean that I am seeking to change God's mind, to dissuade God from a course of hostility or indifference to my cause. It cannot be that my prayer is a treatment plan for God to follow, or a catalogue order form. I am not planning or shopping when I pray.

What I am doing when I pray is loving.

I am aligning myself with the love of God, that energy from which I have come, in which I live and to which I am going. Like the iron filings, I cannot help but leap toward the attractive love of God that pulls me in a constant thread toward connection. Everything that I am longs to be in that stream of power, completely aligned with it so there is no turning to the right or to the left, but straight on in its train. This is true whether or not I am aware of my own longing—the longing was there before my awareness ever appeared.

The energy is infinite. Whether I am large or small makes

no difference. It can carry me or flow through me regardless of my awareness of my own power or lack of it. I can compare prayer to a river—strong, clean, swift, carrying everything along in its powerful current. When I pray, I have stepped into the river and allowed it to carry me. When I pray for you, I have taken your hand and together we step into the river and let it carry us with power.

And when I *don't* pray? When I am indifferent, fallen far away? If someone has no knowledge of faith, nor any interest in it? In spiritual direction, I often speak with a directee about aligning ourselves with the divine will in our prayer intention. You just name the person for whom you pray, I tell them. Just the name. You don't need to spell out the need or provide a lot of information—the name is enough. *It changes you first,* I say, when we speak of this kind of prayer. *It changes the one you are praying for, though you may never know how. And then it changes the world, even if it's just a little bit.*

This can be hard for some people to hear. They feel they should be working harder. *You mean I don't have to do anything? You mean it doesn't matter if I am pure in my intention?*

What about the necessity of making what some Christians call a "full decision for Christ?" There are those who will assert that someone who hasn't made one cannot properly be called a Christian. Perhaps the phrase itself contains a clue to better understanding the love of God—specifically, the word "decision." A decision is a conscious action of the will. Feelings may prompt it and reason may advise it, but the decision is a matter of resolve. The brain makes decisions, but not the whole of the brain: decisions are cognitive. They are the result of thinking.

The part of the brain that decides things is an important part of what makes us human. But it is not the whole. An unborn baby cannot make a full decision for Christ. Neither can a person with a profound developmental disability. A person who is in a coma can't. A toddler can't—the biographies of the saints are full of tales of their exhibiting an adult capacity for faith when they were tiny, but most people view these stories as more admiring than accurate. The conviction that a full decision for Christ is necessary to salvation mistakes a portion of who both God and we are for the whole. When we considered the harrowing of hell, we saw what monstrous propositions can follow from this insistence: little children burning perpetually in a fiery hell because they died before they could make a full decision for Christ (if the writer is evangelical) or before they could be baptized (if the writer is Catholic). But God is free; our errors and limitations cannot impede the infinite energy of existence.

And we are in Christ: the whole of who we are is part of who God is, and this is so even if we only experience it one piece at a time. The trinity of the human being—feelings, reason, and will—lives together, even if we do not always experience its unity within ourselves. Different tasks bring different aspects of us to the fore. We buy real estate and, it is hoped, use our reason in that purchase. We run a marathon and our will carries us to the finish line. Our feelings propel us to fall in love—should we marry, it is hoped that reason will not be entirely absent from the transaction. My decisions never stand alone. Rather than quizzing ourselves and others to determine if our decisions for Christ are full enough, it might be better to say that God is making a full decision in me, and that this decision is playing out my whole life long. My trust can be in the creative power of everything that is. It need not depend on my tiny sliver of it.

CHAPTER 9

ANIMAL, VEGETABLE, MINERAL

Existence is communal. None of us are alone.

Squid swim together in a wedge formation, like geese fly. It aids their speed. Squid swim by jet propulsion—if everyone flies in a wedge, nobody must contend with headwind from anybody else.

Lions hunt in packs. They live in the savannah, wide open grassy space where they have evolved into excellent endurance runners. Tigers don't hunt in packs. They hide in the jungle alone and pounce. They haven't nearly the endurance lions have. House cats, such as we know today, are more like tigers than lions.

Bacteria live in the human gut and on our skin. Most are harmlessly along for the ride, but some are essential to our health and a few are harmful. One of the reasons babies need cuddling is to receive beneficial bacteria from their mothers and anyone else who happens along and wants to snuggle with them.

Honeybees and flowers.

Sloths and green algae. The algae grows in the water that collects on the sloth's fur, and then the sloth eats the algae.

Crocodiles and Egyptian plovers. The birds floss the crocs' teeth.

There are darker tales to tell. A sapling sprouts beneath an oak, born from one of its acorns. It grows. But soon the parent tree sucks up the water and nutrients the sapling needs—it is bigger, with more efficient roots. The sapling withers and dies. Its decomposition nourishes the parent tree.

Some male ants, male bees, male octopuses, male salmon, and certain marsupials die after mating. Though it kills them, they are driven to do it anyway—but you knew that. One of the marsupials, the antechinus, which lives in Australia and looks like a hamster, mates for a solid month straight and then drops dead.

Lichen is an organic duo: an algae and a fungus together. The fungus needs the algae's ability to make food through photosynthesis. The algae attaches to the fungus to give itself a wider range of places in which it can live. Some algae and some fungi can only survive together.

Scientists can't decide whether a virus is organic or inorganic. It doesn't form cells. But it does contain carbon and it has DNA. So it is a missing link between the world of people, plants, and animals and the world of things.

The same is true of crude oil. If it's the product of decomposed plants and animals under pressure, it's one thing. If it comes from carbon deposits deep in the earth, it's another. A mild argument about this has continued off and on since the seventeenth century. Currently, the organic people are winning.

Hair and fingernails are dead, except for the matrix under the skin, from which they grow. Bones are alive. Blood is alive. The insides of teeth are alive, but not the part that shows when you smile.

My friend Katherine, who is a microbiologist, says I'm asking the wrong question. *You don't need to know whether a virus is organic. It's an organic compound. What you're really asking is if it is living. "Living" and "organic" are not synonyms.*

Oh.

So yes, then: my desk is organic because it is made of wood, which came from a tree. But it is no longer living. And a virus is an organic compound that doesn't exhibit all the characteristics of organic life but acts as if it were alive. Sort of.

From a distance, the distinction between alive and not alive seems simple, as does the distinction between life and death. Up close, it is not so clear. Sit next to someone who is dying. His eyes may be closed or open—if they are open, you can tell that he no longer sees you. At the end, you count the seconds between each breath: 4 seconds. 6 seconds. 8 seconds. 9 seconds. 10 seconds. But then you count 11, 12, 15, 20. You search his face. You go on counting. 25 seconds. 30. *Oh*, you say, aloud or to yourself, *he's gone*. You watch for a while longer, but everything is still now. You meet the eyes of another person standing there with you, and a silent message passes between you. *We just saw him leave*. You give a slight nod.

Depart, O Christian soul, out of this world, in the name of God the Father who created you, God the Son who redeemed you, God the Holy Spirit who gave you life.

Less than a minute ago, he was alive. His heart was still beating, as it had since he was about the size of the nail on your little finger. Less than a minute ago the blood still trickled weakly through his veins and arteries, his chest still rose and fell slightly with his failing breath. You sat there and watched as it slowed and then stopped, and now it seems that it would be a small matter to start everything up again—heart, blood, lungs. It seems that you could just rewind and there he would be, back in his body again. Could that not be done? How could life be here one moment and gone the next, you ask yourself as a nurse begins to move quietly in and out of the room. His body is right there, looking just as it did a minute ago. But its character has completely changed. He has departed from it. He has changed states.

Other life, microscopic life, will begin in the place where he lived. It already has; it began before he left. Many people—most people—think of this fact as dreadful, view his body as monstrous now. It isn't monstrous, though; it's just natural. Some are afraid to be alone with him. There is no need for that. We have much more to fear from the living.

What constitutes his body is changing. Depending on what his family decides, there are several things that might happen to it. If he is to be embalmed, the undertaker will go to great lengths to slow the process by which his body returns to nourish the earth, preserving his soft tissues with chemicals that may prevent their decomposition for years. Nobody living will be able to admire this, of course, unless his body is exhumed for some reason. If he is not embalmed, his decomposition will proceed more quickly—but his reunion with the earth may still be prevented, because the cemetery requires that his coffin be enclosed within a cement vault to protect it—protect it from what, I have never understood. I believe what a grave vault protects is actually the cemetery lawn from settling, keeping it level and thus easier for the lawn care people to mow. Certainly the person in the coffin is in no need of protection.

If he is to be cremated, his remains can be placed directly into the ground and he can continue the joyful journey of which the life you knew was just an era, one of many eras. Because life, with all its heartaches, is a joyful journey. Existence is good, existence of whatever kind, animal, vegetable or mineral. The earth is good. It is good to be a part of it again. Living or dead. Organic or inorganic. If you happen to be there when I die, tell them that I want to be cremated and get to work renewing the earth as soon as possible. Tell them that I was an enthusiastic gardener. You might mention that our garden was once on a garden tour.

> All we go down to the dust.
> Yet even at the grave, we make our song.
> Alleluia. Alleluia. Alleluia.[1]

Kate the cat lived to be nineteen. *She's no better?* the young lady at the vet's office asked. We stood in the waiting room. I held her bony little body, wrapped for the trip in a soft towel. We hadn't wanted to put her in her cat carrier: She detested it even in the best of times. I shook my head no, and Q did the same. We could not speak for sorrow. Soon we were in the treatment room with her, listening to the vet explain what would happen. First he would give her a sedative, then a shot directly into her heart to stop it. She would feel nothing.

A tiny bit of dark blood crept back up into the syringe when the injection was finished. *You did the right thing,* he said then. We nodded, still not trusting our voices. We took her back home. Q dug a hole and buried her in the flower bed, still wrapped in her towel. We said a prayer and planted some daffodil bulbs over her, to come up in the spring.

---

1 Kantakion, the chant used for the burial of the dead in the Orthodox Christian tradition. This English translation is the one used in the Episcopal Church's 1979 Book of Common Prayer.

When I am in the ground, there will be no difference between Kate and me. There wasn't all that much when she was here, really, just differences in certain talents and certain abilities. I could speak and write English and she couldn't, but she had ways of knowing things about other cats that I could not fathom. She could jump straight up onto a surface four times as high as she was, something I could not do if my life depended on it. She could see in the dark and I can't, but I can drive a stick shift and she couldn't. She could catch a mouse and I can open a can.

We were different. But we were made of the same stuff. My constituent atoms, formed of the energy of creation like everything else, were arranged to form me. Kate perceived the order of me through the lens of who she was. I did the same with her. Nobody else knew her as I knew her, and I did not know her as my husband knew her, though we both met her at precisely the same time in precisely the same place. Their cosmic arrangement was between the two of them. But we also were a trio, the little cat and the two of us, so we constructed that arrangement as well—she was herself with us, and we were ourselves with her. Together, we were us. People came and went in our lives, and in time we came and went ourselves. All of us, all who came and went, were part of the arrangement of energy that was us. We linked all the parts of it together with memory so that we could make sense of all the energy, all the molecules, all the cells, all the atoms, all the electrical impulses. Just as linear time is a model we create so that we can manage our lives, and matter is a model we create so that we can perceive the energy of the universe, love as we know it is a model, too. We take the love of God—infinite energy, existence itself—and package it into manageable units, small enough for us to encompass.

> "If I come to the people of Israel and say to them, 'The God of your fathers has sent me to you,' and they ask me, 'What is his name?' what shall I say to them?" God said to Moses, "I am who I am."[2]

I don't imagine that "I am" made much sense to the Hebrews back then. People want a name and a shape for everything, so we construct names and shapes for everything we experience. The biblical writers constructed, too: a name and a shape for themselves, and—over the centuries—many names and shapes for God. They constructed a king, with a royal court. They constructed a military leader. Certainly they constructed a Father God—once in a great while they even constructed a Mother God! They imagined God the Lover, God the Physician, God the Professor, the Architect, the Builder, the Potter, the Shepherd—they pictured God as a participant in every social relation human beings know about. But in this seminal first encounter with Moses, none of those images sufficed.

Interesting: all this literary picturing of God in all these different ways notwithstanding, Jews have maintained a prohibition against the visual representation of God in worship basing it on a reading of the second of the ten commandments (which was really a prohibition against worshipping idols representing *other* gods, household gods such as the ones mentioned in Genesis 31, not the God of Israel). To this day, an observant Jew in a conservative tradition won't even speak the word "God"—she will say something like "Master of the Universe, Blessed be He" instead. In writing, she will hyphenate it, "G-d", so as not to tread upon it. The interesting work of specifically representing God in art would be largely left for their Christian descendants. Who is to say how many fantastical gods the Hebrews left behind them in Egypt—gods with enormous

2 Exod. 3:13–14.

wings, gods with the heads of birds and cats. How many did they encounter along the way to the promised land? Who knows how many tempted them to their worship once they got there? We do know that they sometimes yielded to that temptation—the prophets and historians of Israel would not have excoriated the people for sacrificing to idols if they hadn't been doing it.

The austerity we have inherited from Israel's rejection of iconic representation of God has a use when we consider the *alsolife*: It calls us to rise above our constructions. Every time we name something, we are constructing it. Our perception of the shape and location of everything is approximate. The energy of creation is too much for us to handle; we must corral it into manageable pieces. I cannot bear the molecular motion of my desk, the cellular buzz that is my cat; I cannot even bear the roar of energy within my own body. So my mind finds a way not to know about those things. I edit my reality. I take my perception of everything I encounter, and I call it the whole.

Is this a modern viewpoint? I am a modern person, but here is a psalmist writing three thousand years ago, who sings about a reality "too wonderful for me," about the experience of the universe that unites things which cannot be joined, that surrounds, predates and follows everything we perceive, including ourselves. This is a psalm about the *alsolife*. It is *kairos*: both before and after everything.

> O Lord, you have searched me and known me.
> You know when I sit down and when I rise up;
>   you discern my thoughts from far away.
> You search out my path and my lying down,
>   and are acquainted with all my ways.
> Even before a word is on my tongue,
>   O Lord, you know it completely.
> You hem me in, behind and before,
>   and lay your hand upon me.

Such knowledge is too wonderful for me;
  it is so high that I cannot attain it.
Where can I go from your spirit?
  Or where can I flee from your presence?
If I ascend to heaven, you are there;
  if I make my bed in Sheol, you are there.
If I take the wings of the morning
  and settle at the farthest limits of the sea,
even there your hand shall lead me,
  and your right hand shall hold me fast.
If I say, "Surely the darkness shall cover me,
  and the light around me become night,"
even the darkness is not dark to you;
  the night is as bright as the day,
  for darkness is as light to you.
For it was you who formed my inward parts;
  you knit me together in my mother's womb.
I praise you, for I am fearfully and wonderfully made.
  Wonderful are your works;
that I know very well.
  My frame was not hidden from you,
when I was being made in secret,
  intricately woven in the depths of the earth.
Your eyes beheld my unformed substance.
In your book were written
  all the days that were formed for me,
  when none of them as yet existed.
How weighty to me are your thoughts, O God!
  How vast is the sum of them!
I try to count them—they are more than the sand;
  I come to the end—I am still with you.[3]

3 Ps. 139:1–18.

I imagine the composition of this song. Is he sitting on a hilltop at night? Are the stars leaning out of the heavens, seeming so close that he might pluck one, as they were that night when I was walking back to the monastery and stopped in my tracks to gaze at them? Did he feel himself carried from the very large to the very small, moving from the vastness of interstellar space to the tiny beginning of his own life? Did they seem somehow the same to him, as they sometimes do to me? And did he have the language to describe this? No, not completely; the amazingness of the heavens overwhelmed him, and it was unspeakable. But what language he had, he used, as I do. As you do.

We often use this psalm at funerals. At a funeral, I do two things: I remember the life and I suggest the *alsolife*. People need and deserve to hear what a blessing the one they loved was to the world, what a blessing she still is. And people need to hear something about what life is like for her now, at a time when they feel the need to hear it. The *alsolife* is true all the time, but we don't care all that much about it until we need it, and that's when we lose someone we love. When the five-fold "Never" enters our brain and won't go away. When we have nothing earthly to clasp to ourselves, but need to clasp something. That is the time when we need to hear that everything that ever was still is. That the resurrection is now, not some time in the distant future. We need to know that the love we shared has not come to an end, that the power of it goes on and on and continues to strengthen us. We need to hear that the beloved dead are stronger and more mobile now than they ever were when they walked the earth with us, because now they are in Christ. We need to know that life has not been a test to determine whether or not we qualify for the timeless love of God. We need not qualify for God's love—we are made of it.

I always tell them to stay tuned. I tell them that love never ends, that the energy of the one they love has not gone anywhere, and that they may experience it. If they do, it will not be in the old way—they don't call, they don't write. I tell them that it may come to them in a dream, or a stray thought, or some silly coincidence that would have no meaning at all to anyone else. I tell them that this doesn't matter, it's not *for* anyone else. I tell them that God, who is the energy of creation, uses the thoughts and memories we have, as God uses everything else. Space dust we were and space dust we are and space dust we will be. *All we go down to the dust. Yet even at the grave we make our song. Alleluia! Alleluia! Alleleuia!*

CHAPTER 10

THE TWO BASKETS

In lower Manhattan's Museum of Jewish Heritage hangs a long canvas painted with dozens of fanciful designs. It covers two walls of one room. Animals, flowers, houses, and street scenes of early twentieth century Budapest adorn it. It took Aryeh Steinberger years to complete. He worked on it throughout the 1920s and 1930s and used it to line his family's Succah, the tent-like structure they built every year outside their house. The family stayed in the booth during the autumn harvest festival, a ritual memory of the Israelites' time in the wilderness as they made their way to the promised land.

Aryeh Steinberger, *Waiting for a Minhyan*,
Budapest, ca. 1920–30

His children must have adored it. We know they did, because they buried it beneath their synagogue to keep it safe during the Holocaust, and went back to Budapest to retrieve it when the war was over. It was displayed in the Brooklyn apartment of Mr. Steinberger's daughter until she donated it to the museum in 1997. Of course they loved it—it was a tangible artifact of their father's presence in their happy home, a piece of a world now gone forever.

All kids love to make tents—it was a favorite rainy day activity for my girls when they were little. There is no end to the pretending one can do inside a makeshift cave of sheets and blankets draped over chairs and tables. Reality is outside; it dictates its own terms, and we all must abide by them. In our tent, though, anything can happen!

It must have been beautiful inside that family's Sukkah, the candlelight washing the brightly colored walls. It must have been a place of stories, lots of them, real stories and magical made-up ones. It must have been a place of safety, a safety real or bravely imagined—Eastern Europe in the 1930s soon would not be a safe place at all. The children must have remembered their father's Sukkah long into their own adulthood. Every year they must have unrolled and hung it, marveling as they did so at their father's imagination and his astounding patience.

Aryeh Steinberger's Sukkah reminds me of something. I think of it when I struggle to describe the timeless life that surrounds the life we live, so conditioned and limited by the fact that it is passing away. It is beautiful here. We are safe here. We love it here.

This is the perennial sorrow of humanity: we love it here, but we cannot stay.

Aryeh Steinberger, *Succah*, Budapest, ca. 1920–30

Chronos.

Listen:

It is as if there were two baskets, one large and one small. The smaller one sits inside the larger one.

We live in the smaller one. It is this world. I don't mean this world, planet Earth—I mean this universe, the whole thing. The existence we know. We love it here, love everything about it. It is beautiful to us.

It is like the mural Aryeh Steinberger made for his family's Sukkah—everywhere we turn, there is beauty. Everyone and everything we love are here. The smallest crumbs of its history and our history in it fascinate us: we snap photos of it, haunt the library and the Internet to learn about its past, watch its birds and its butterflies, don goggles and rubber flippers to swim with its fish. We wish we could have seen the dinosaurs. At times, our memories of the past fill us with longing for it. Sometimes they make us weep.

More than anything else, we fear leaving the smaller basket—most of us cannot bear even to contemplate leaving. When someone leaves, we count it a great sorrow. To us, the basket is wounded by the loss of even one of us. There is a hole in it, and so there is a hole in us. It takes a long time to recover. Some of us never do.

Baskets are woven, of course: Strips of grass or straw or wood thread intricately over and under one another again and again, to create a concave form. But there is space between the strips, however tightly they might be woven. You could peer out one of those spaces, if you wanted to. Maybe you do, once or twice—put your eye right up against the opening and squint. Yup, there's something out there, all right. But you can't see it very clearly through that tiny opening.

Besides, who cares? The basket you're in is beautiful. It contains everything you need.

One day, though, the smaller basket begins to fall apart. *This is it,* you tell yourself, and fear grips you: This is the moment you have dreaded all your life, the one of which you have refused to think—this is the moment when you must leave your beloved basket behind. It is difficult. Painful, perhaps. But you must go. Soon you become more and more intent on your leaving, impelled there, less and less interested in staying. You see that this is hard on the people around you who love you, but you can't help it. It is too hard to stay. At last the smaller basket falls away completely, and you stand amid its shards.

You look around you. You realize that you have seen this place before.

Ah, now you remember! *This is the place I saw that time when I was trying to look out through the wall of my basket. This is what was all around us, only we didn't pay any attention to it. I have always been here.*

We have always been there.

We have already noticed that when Jesus talks about the kingdom of heaven, he often does so in the present tense: not "The kingdom of heaven will be" but "The kingdom of heaven IS"—*The kingdom of God IS within you . . . the kingdom of heaven IS like a mustard seed . . . the kingdom of heaven IS like yeast . . . the kingdom of heaven IS like a treasure hidden in a field.*[1] The kingdom is not just a future reality. It is a current one.

And clearly, it is not a place, in any geographical sense of the word. It's not a place to which we go. We are there already—*I have always been here.* Our notions of the life larger than this life are cripplingly provincial, utterly conditioned by the limited parameters of the smaller basket. The very term "kingdom of heaven" is an example of this parochialism, conjuring as it does the image of a royal court in biblical times: it is unlikely that the ground of all being much resembles an ancient Near

1 Luke 17:21,Matt. 13:31, 33, 44.

Eastern potentate. Or, as Jesus put it, *My kingdom is not of this world.*[2] When we use such a term, we come face-to-face with the limitation of religious language and are reminded once again that all of it is metaphor—the things of God cannot be contained by our words or images. At their very best, they can never be more than approximations. This is not to suggest that we should refrain from speaking of God at all—only to recommend a realistic humility when we do.

The smaller basket has collapsed around you. You are in the larger basket now, as you have always been and didn't know it. For the first time, you see it clearly.

This larger basket is the *alsolife.* Containing all existence, "all in all" as Paul put it, the *alsolife* is what you might have grown up calling the "afterlife." But that term leaves us needing more: the linear time line upon which the notion of an afterlife stands breaks down against the backdrop of the elasticity of time. God cannot have time as we understand it. We experience linear time here in the smaller basket—we need it to experience our life, to experience the way reality works in a way we can handle. Remember how Albert Einstein described God's simultaneous past, present, and future: *Time,* he said, *is what we have so that everything doesn't happen all at once.* What the ancients called the kingdom of God cannot begin at the end of an earthly time line. It must be without end, as you were taught, but it must also be without beginning—if there is a time before the kingdom of God, that cannot be the kingdom of God. There can be no time when God was not. Rather than a point on a line, the *alsolife* must surround this and all other lives—it must be more spherical than linear. It must be like the larger basket.

Remember the stars with which we began this book. Recall that some them aren't there anymore. Weren't there when you were looking right at them. You knew this already, of course,

2 John 18:36.

from your school days. We only see the stars at all because they emit light—if stars didn't shine, all we would see when we looked up would be the blackness of space. But light does shine from them, and it travels toward us, and we behold a star. Except that the star we see now is not the star in its current form—the light that hits our eyes today left that star years ago, millennia ago. It took that long for the light to reach us. Who knows what that star really is now, at the moment you are seeing it. It might still be burning, but a lot of time has passed. That star could have done whatever it is that stars do when they end it all. It might not be there now.

You are seeing that star's past—in your present.

This fact provides a hint of what time is like in that existence which contains our existence. Linear time is earthly, and it is relative to the one experiencing it. Linear time exists in proportion to spatial existence: it's about getting from one place to another, from one state to another. Linear time measures change. *Chronos*.

But say you are God, and hold the whole of the universe's history? What if you author existence itself? You, God, can experience no loss with passage of time, for there can be no moment from which you are absent. Everything for you must be now. What we know as *duration* is the stringing out of what is actually a moment. This is the only way we can hold what actually is: one moment at a time. We can't experience it all at once, so we hold it in bite-sized pieces.

Time is what we have so that everything doesn't happen all at once. But the truth is, everything *does* happen all at once. God can experience this. Tethered as we are to the earth, we cannot.

So? Is this approach to time of any use, or is it merely interesting? It is more than merely interesting for me. The elasticity of time is profoundly comforting.

Here is why: We see everything in terms of our experience. My hearing a sound is part of the sound, my seeing participates in the existence of what I see. All things behave as electricity behaves: no power experienced until the circuit completes and then, there it is.

Remember that we imagined the faraway star's experience, if our perspectives were reversed. We imagined a race superior to our own, on one of the planets in that star's solar system, a race whose telescopes were far more advanced than any we have—able to see the planets move around our sun, able to see our planet Earth, to pick out our location on it, so powerful that they could even see me. They would look and there I would be, sitting in the garden watching the hummingbirds feed, writing on my iPad.

Except that by the time they saw me, I would have been dead for thousands of years. Our house, long gone. This garden, this town—no more. The Earth, too, probably. They would be seeing my past in their present, looking into ancient history and seeing it live and move: a woman of ancient times, living and moving right before their eyes.

Comforting, yes—because what is our greatest sorrow? That everything slides inexorably into the past. And our greatest dread? Sliding there ourselves, we and everything we adore—every person, every dog and cat and bird, every building and every city, all slipping away from us. No matter how we try, we can hold onto none of it. Our very measuring of it is painful. How much longer do I have, we wonder. Each day brings us closer to the end.

So think of it: somebody, somewhere, somebody far away, with the right kind of telescope—somebody could see us still! The light reflecting from us hurtles into space, crosses light-years and light-years, light-centuries, light-millennia—and reaches someone. Somebody sees you, when you are four and your mother is combing your hair. Somebody sees your parents meet for the first time. Sees your *grandparents* meet. Somewhere, William Shakespeare finishes *The Winter's Tale* and puts down his pen. The images of our past shoot through space until they are perceived. Yes, they are images. Reflected light. But we don't just reflect energy in the form of light; we also emanate energy. Not a lot—we are not very big. But we are composed of energy, the frantic motion of our constituent molecules and the motion of their constituent atoms invisible to the naked eye but very real. Energy holds us together, and energy is never destroyed. It may change form, but it does not disappear. It can be detected, however faintly, forever.

But I don't want it to change form! I want it to stay in the same form!

No, you don't, for you will have changed form yourself. You would not be here to perceive your universe, even if it did remain in its current form. You would have moved on. Move on! Everything you have ever loved is in the larger basket, as it has always been. It is all waiting for you. It is all in the Now of God.

The dead are all there. You are there, too, though you do not yet perceive it: the *you* of now and the *you* of the past are there. The you of the future is there, too. Perhaps even the you that might have been is there, the infinite possibilities of your *youness* besides the one that our world knows, which we are naive enough to think is the Real You. You are not just the *you* of the facts of your life as you know them; you are also the *you* of its possibilities. Do we imagine that Osama bin Laden or Adolf Hitler could only have been what they became? That their evil was inevitable? Do we imagine that their evil was greater than the power of the whole world's existence?

Our existence is born in the imagination of God, that great well of possibility that dwarfs our own imagining. What falls short of it in the sad linearity of *chronos* need not do so in the more generous and immediate simultaneity of the *alsolife*. Sometimes the fullness of time breaks into our day-to-day sorrows: a miracle happens and we see it. But even if we don't, the possibility of it is there. All of it.

The good news—do you see it yet? What the *alsolife* means is that nothing is lost.

This is resurrection. It is not the resuscitation of only one small strand of your life.

It is the realization of all of it.

And not yours only, or mine only. It is the fulfillment of all of us who have ever lived.

There is no past. It is all now.

World without end.

And let all creation say, Amen.

CPSIA information can be obtained
at www.ICGtesting.com
Printed in the USA
LVOW01s1332210317
527804LV00010B/167/P